The God Questions

What Forms and Shapes Us

PATRICK J. RUSSELL

Liguori

LIGUORI, MISSOURI

Imprimi Potest: Thomas D. Picton, C.Ss.R.
Provincial, Denver Province • The Redemptorists

Published by Liguori Publications • Liguori, Missouri
www.liguori.org

Library of Congress Cataloging-in-Publication Data

Russell, Patrick J.
    The God questions: what forms and shapes us / Patrick J. Russell. —
1st ed.
      p. cm.
    Includes bibliographical references.
    ISBN 978-0-7648-1629-1
    1. Spirituality. 2. Mississippi River Valley—Discovery and exploration. 3. Russell, Patrick J. 4. Marquette, Jacques, 1637–1675. I. Title.
    BV4501.3.R8 2007
    248—dc22   2007934356

The author and publisher gratefully acknowledge permission to reprint/reproduce copyrighted works granted by the publishers/sources listed on pages 171–172.

Liguori Publications, a nonprofit corporation, is an apostolate of the Redemptorists. To learn more about the Redemptorists, visit Redemptorists.com.

Printed in the United States of America
11 10 09 08 07 5 4 3 2 1
First edition

To my father, Edmund P. Russell, Jr.,
who taught me to see goodness in all things and people,
and to my wife, Stephanie Rossiter Russell,
who is goodness personified and the love of my life.

Contents

Introduction

Stormy Time

It was a dark and stormy night. Really, it was, which was odd. Not the dark part; after all, this was early January in Wisconsin where it gets dark by 4:00 PM, but the storm...rain, thunder, lightning. Odd. It should be cold and snowing, which would be better than this bone-chilling dampness. Not a night to be out. Getting out of my car, bracing myself against the lashing wind and the wintry rain, I dashed into a large discount store.

It was the night before the Feast of Epiphany and I was here to buy a gift. Actually, four gifts, but the same item. Four canoe paddles. One paddle for each of my four sons.

The paddles were part of a plan. My eldest son was graduating from college in the spring and moving to New York City in midsummer. My other three sons also were no longer boys but on the cusp of manhood. The second oldest would become a legal adult when he turned twenty-one in the coming year. The next oldest would be eligible for his driver's license that coming spring. Even the youngest had become a teenager the previous fall. I was no longer the dad of four boys; I was the father of young men. Time was rushing by—and it was carrying my sons with it.

So I had resolved during Advent that the next summer I would follow through with a plan that had been brewing within me for some time. In fact, five years earlier I made an aborted effort to implement it. Even this year, I had meant to give these paddles at Christmas, but I never got around to buying them. Epiphany is a time for gift-giving, so I was determined not to let it pass without giving these gifts and launching my plan. Time demanded action.

The plan? With each son accompanying me on a separate leg, we would re-enact part of one of the most historic and intrepid journeys from the earliest years of European exploration of the New World. By undertaking a roughly 100-mile canoe trip down the Wisconsin River to its confluence with the Mississippi River, we would relive the 1673 expedition of Father Jacques Marquette and Louis Jolliet down this same river in their successful quest to discover a great river that was reputed, according to Native American legends, to flow to the Immense Waters—the Sea. The Marquette-Jolliet exploration of the Mississippi River and journey into the heart of the North American continent was one of the great moments in the history of the "new world."

God Questions

This book recounts this canoe trip with my sons, but it is primarily about everyone's universal journey—our voyage *into* God. The river teaches us that the journey is as important as the destination; that our anxious questionings are as important as the answers; that our faith is as important as our destination—God. With respect to our spiritual journey, God seems to be more about questions than answers. Theologically speaking, God is question(s) *and* answer(s), the alpha *and* the omega.

On the river (of life), we start our spiritual journey by seeking the questions—the twists, turns, and unexpected surprises—not the answers. This, of course, is not how some religious denominations often present the journey of faith. I once saw a billboard that shouted: "GOD IS THE ANSWER!" *But what is the question*, I wondered. As Johnny Carson's old "Carnac" routine so humorously made clear, the answer doesn't make any sense without first knowing the question. The *Jeopardy* game show, which requires an answer in the form of a question, expresses a fundamental reality: it is very perilous to think that we can know the answer(s) if we don't first ask the question(s).

This book is about more than a canoe trip with my four sons. It is *not* merely a record of events. Rather, it is about the questions we discovered, the questions everyone seems to encounter in life—*the God Questions*. These are the questions that we need to help our children, and ourselves, to "see" in the life around us if we are to have any hope of discovering the Answer (God). There are an infinite number of questions on the road to God, but four of them, symbolized here by the four canoe paddles, in particular, propel most journeys:

What is our place in the world?
Who is God calling us to be?
How is God caring for us?
Where is God's love?

God forms and shapes us by these very questions. Just as their typographical appearance on the page narrows from one sentence to the next, these questions pull us in and taper us; they focus on the ultimate point of our existence. But they don't constrict us, they "contract" us, for they are the pangs through which God gives birth to a new creation.

The difference between *constriction* and *contraction* is only one small consonant and one measly vowel, but in the spiritual quest the distinction is huge. Too often people perceive faith as being about restricting life: controlling and managing it by eliminating those things that threaten and tempt us. Religion, done in this vein, is all about the "NO's." Do *not* do this! Do *not* do that! But faith is really an invitation: an invitation by God to enter into the fullness of life. Not surprisingly, then, faith is about the "YES's"—responding to God's summons to open doors into the

unknown. This process leads to ever-new thresholds of love. Constriction is about staying put; contraction is about going forth.

Those of us who are parents know about birth contractions.
Biological mothers know this more intimately and profoundly
than the rest of us. Fathers who have been present at their child's
birth have indirectly experienced birth contractions through their
feelings for their partner as she pushes new life into being. Even
those who have never been present at a birth (for example, those
who have adopted a child or who have even just loved a child)
know about birth contractions in a very real, tangible, and actual
way. Because giving birth to our children is not a one-time event
of emerging from the womb; it is a lifelong process. We constantly
"give birth" to our children as we strive to fashion and form them,
prod and protect them, comfort and console them, discipline and
adore them.

Even those who are not parents know about birth contractions, because we have all been—and still are—children. We have
all been birthed in love...hopefully by our parents, but certainly
by God. So all of us know about birth contractions. And thus
all of us should know about the God Questions, even if only
intuitively.

Discovery Journey

This book uses one river journey as a metaphor for the voyage that
every life takes through the contractions of the God Questions.
This particular river, the Wisconsin River, was deliberately chosen
because of its historical significance. It is sometimes called the
"River of Discovery" because by following this river Marquette
and Jolliet became the first Europeans to lay eyes on the Mississippi River flowing through the heart of the North American
continent. The Marquette-Jolliet journey is rightly immortalized
in every fifth-grade history textbook, particularly since the Mis-

sissippi River is one of the most significant rivers in the United States. Even before the last states were established, the Mississippi was the commercial bloodstream of North America. Even more important, it became the spiritual lifeblood that united the nation. As a geographical feature, it separated East from West. After the Civil War, it became the lifeline that restored the bond between the disparate cultures of North and South. The paddle-wheelers and showboats plied their trades up and down its shores while people from many nations examined the new territory. On its banks was born the prose of Mark Twain, who literarily articulated the emerging identity of a young nation. The heart of America pumped into (and out of) the Mississippi River.

Thus a canoe trip reenacting the Marquette-Jolliet passage ignited my historical imagination and seemed particularly *apropos* for my family. My four sons had graduated from, were attending, or would be students at Marquette University High School, named after the Jesuit missionary and explorer. Furthermore, my wife and I had earned our undergraduate degrees from Marquette University. I went on to earn my doctorate from Marquette University, and my wife presently works there. So retracing the steps of Marquette's historic accomplishment seemed a natural choice.

Other aspects of this canoe trip also were attractive. This particular stretch of the Wisconsin River is noteworthy; it is the longest free-flowing stretch (uninterrupted by dams) of navigable river in the Midwest. Its pristine and natural beauty is protected by an enlightened state law that inhibits man-made development and has transferred most of the shoreline to public ownership. With minimal signs of human presence, the tree-lined river's scenic appeal is well appreciated in the majestic bluffs cradling the river, the lush islands dotting the waterway, and the frequent sightings of bald eagles, waterfowl, and other wildlife. Canoeists can camp on any of the river's sandbar islands, so the journey truly feels like a wilderness adventure.

Beyond the interesting historical connections and captivating ascetic beauty, even the river's name (Wisconsin) seemed to presage well for this trip. The word *Wisconsin* derives from a Native American word that means "the gathering of waters." Taking the trip in four stages with each son accompanying me for a different leg would allow me time to "gather" with each son individually and talk about important things...things connected to the God Questions. For contained in the God Questions is a spiritual paradigm or life map for the journey down the river of life. By retreating to a great moment in time, experiencing the beauty of nature, and engaging in intentional conversation our experience will certainly have to bear something of the deep mystery that connects our lives to the Great River of Life's Purpose or the Massive Sea of Love.

Gathering Water

I readily admit that this plan stemmed in part from a bit of desperation. In the heart of every parent is an unsettling question: How do I set my children on the right path so that they will truly find happiness in life? Implementing proper discipline techniques, building self-esteem, promoting good study habits, picking the right college, and even developing a superstar athlete like Tiger Woods—these are the tasks that the world prioritizes for us as parents. They are important life skills (well, maybe not the Tiger thing) that help our children be successful, but they don't directly address the thing that lies at the very center of human happiness: the spiritual odyssey.

Unfortunately, there is no simple answer, no magic wand, no ten-step program to happiness, which is our shorthand term for living the authentic, fulfilling life. In fact, as suggested previously, the key to happiness is not so much a matter of providing answers as it is recognizing God's grand pattern in our anxious (and not-so-anxious) questions.

So there's the rub. The answer to life's questions is no answer at all, but an orientation, a stance, a perspective. That means it is not hard and fast, but soft and elusive. It is more about distinguishing the undercurrents of life's movements than building a monument to one's accomplishments. Hmm, it's like *water*. Between 50 and 75 percent of our body's composition is water: a whopping 83 percent of our blood, 75 percent of our muscle, and even 22 percent of our bones is water. The only part of our body that doesn't contain water is fat, which figures (pun intended!). In essence, we are water people.

Yet, have you ever attempted to cup water in your hands and pass it to another person? Impossible! Only a dribble remains. The same thing happens in trying to cup the fundamental spiritual "something" that is so important to living a happy, fulfilling, authentic life. Like water, it cannot be grasped in the hand but rather is intrinsically integrated within the core of one's being. So essential and yet so elusive! Given this reality, how does one describe it, teach it, or pass it on? In a way, we don't; all we can do is point to things that point to it. That is, we point through signs and symbols and in sacraments and scenery. All we can really do is put our children—and ourselves—in a position to see the glimpses of graced moments in our anxious questionings.

I could not think of a better place to possibly catch a glimpse of the power of the God Questions than on a river because of the paradoxical nature of water. Lao Tse, the founder of Taoism, possibly phrased it most provocatively:

> *Nothing in the world is weaker and softer than water.*
> *Yet nothing is its equal in wearing away*
> *   the hard and strong.*
> *Thus the weak overcomes the strong;*
> *   the soft overcomes the hard.*
> *Every person knows this,*
> *   yet no one lives this in practice.*

We prefer hard answers to soft questions; strong beliefs to yielding love. Yet, if we are indeed water people, then God is going to work with us in the way God has made us. So we must seek God in the watery, soft, yielding questions that relentlessly push on our crusty, hard, firm hearts so that God can make them—ever so slowly and patiently—pliable and tender enough to beat with a new spirit. We are reborn through the soft and yielding contractions of the God Questions. Just as we emerged from the waters of our mother's womb, we are born anew through the waters of the God Questions.

Epiphany Paddles

The four paddles were my Epiphany gifts to announce our summer canoe expedition down the Wisconsin River. So on the day after the "stormy night" (the eve of Epiphany), I gathered my sons after dinner to give each one his gift. I was anxious about how they would receive the canoe trip. Would they be excited or unreceptive? Although we traditionally enjoyed family camping, this trip was different.

As I scrambled for the appropriate words and proper time, I could not help but recall another stormy night during a camping trip with my two youngest sons. It was midweek and we were in an out-of-the-way campground as the sole campers in the park. The trip started in glorious, hot-baked, sun-drenched fashion. Suddenly, as we enjoyed swimming in the cool lake, the weather shifted and ill-omened rain clouds darkened the sky. Then the sheets of water came. And came! We retreated to our camper to play cards and wait out the storm, which did not subside until late into the night. During the break in the weather, we headed for an overdue visit to the restrooms. On this moonless summer night, the darkness enveloped us, The only light guiding our steps was our lantern. Odd thing about lanterns: they only shed a circle of light large enough to guide your next step or two. You progress by stepping into that edge of light. As you take a step, the light moves on. Ominous noises might be heard off the trail in the woods, but the lantern—unlike a flashlight—cannot be pointed away from the bearer to shed light on the undergrowth's dark crevasses. It can only show you where you are, not where you are going. Hence, using a lantern to light your way is rather simple: just keep walking to the edge of that ever-moving illuminated circle, trusting that being cradled in a handful of light is enough for this journey.

That was the case for me as I stood before my sons on the first Sunday of a new calendar year during the Feast of Epiphany, a day when we celebrate the guiding light of God. Like the camping lantern, the heavenly star casts a circle of light that does not reveal our entire path. All we can do is step toward the edge of the light and trust that more light will be given. The gospel reading from Matthew during Mass that day told of the Wise Men who followed a tail of starlight with unwavering trust toward Jesus. Despite their best instincts to seek answers in the geometry of the sky (the gospel writer probably pictured them as Zoroastrian astronomers) and to assume that God did not exist in material things (human or other), the Wise Men began to ask the questions that would lead them to find God in the unexpected—human form. No doubt, their Zoroastrian socks were knocked off when the great star from heaven led them to pitiful Bethlehem. Even greater shock must have burst on their faces when the edge of their starlight lantern suddenly revealed their ultimate destination: a little baby!

Armed with the Epiphany of the Wise Men, and the assurance that God would appear at the edge of my lantern, I prepared to announce our river journey and its theological significance to my sons. However, suddenly I was overwhelmed by the concrete challenge of Epiphany. How can we explain such a journey? The questions that must have been exploding in the minds of the Magi! They may have started with "Why's." *Why* did God have us travel for months to arrive at this backwater, godforsaken place just to see nothing but a little baby? *Why* did God call us here just to dash our hopes and lead us to disappointment? *Why* does God care so little for us that he played this cruel joke on us? We've faithfully fulfilled every obligation that God has demanded of us, so *why* doesn't God show his love for us? The Three Wise Guys, as I sometimes like to call them, arrived at the "when" moment—when God manifested himself most fully and completely—and they might well have missed it at first because they jumped right past the other interrogatives, *what, who, how,* and *where,* to get to "WHY?"

We are not much different. Most of us leap right to the *why* whenever we question our faith journey, especially when the question is prompted by a crisis. When someone dies, we ask *why* they had to die. When we hit a midlife crisis or life seems to lack meaning, we ask *why*, and then we fail to listen. When we see our loved ones suffer from rejection, illness, or failure, we ask *why* a good God would allow such bad things to happen. When we feel hurt, alone, and isolated, we ask *why* God doesn't make others love us better.

But the Three Wise Men came to faith. Maybe they backtracked a bit and peered into the cavernous crack that exists between "when" and "why." I would guess they looked at their experience and, maybe for the first time, asked for themselves the God Questions in light of this destabilizing stable encounter.

- In light of what I am seeing in this child Jesus in front of me, what is our place in the world?
- Given the long journey to Bethlehem that we have undertaken, who is God calling us to be?
- Seeing this mother named Mary tenderly caressing this child, how is God caring for us?
- Trusting enough to step into the light's edge, where is God's love?

Using the lens of their own experience as the preface to their questions, now the Magi's questions had the power to unfold their hearts to a new answer. Now the irreconcilable all merged...the divine was now human! These followers of the night star were not only challenged to move beyond the light of their own country, but also beyond their own preconceived ideas about the very reality of their daily world. The foreign visitors discovered Emmanuel: God-is-with-us. I had not yet defined how I could translate this epiphany to my sons, but I sensed the need to merely start the journey.

God calls us to continue journeying past the boundary of our lantern's light. God has more to offer us. We don't have it all. No one has it all. Only God has it, and God is giving it to us. So we are called at every Epiphany to arise and move beyond discouragement, beyond complacency, beyond satisfaction to be open and receptive to all that God is giving us, even when it blows apart our strong assumptions and especially our hard answers! It was time.

With my four sons before me, I gave each one a canoe paddle and announced the plan for the "Russell River Rendezvous," the moniker I had chosen for our canoe trip. I excitedly talked about the connections with Marquette's expedition and the natural beauty of the river. My sons' reactions ranged from mild excitement to pliant acquiescence. But they asked all the right questions. *When* will we go? *What* will the trip entail? *Who* will go at what time? *How* will we work out the details of getting a canoe and packing supplies? *Where* is this river? None of them asked *why.* We were off to a very good start.

PATRICK J. RUSSELL

CHAPTER ONE

What Is Our Place in the World?

What is our place in the world?
Who is God calling us to be?
How is God caring for us?
Where is God's love?

Memorial Gratitude

The launch of the Russell River Rendezvous was scheduled for Memorial Day. I was glad to begin during the last days of May since Marquette began his famous Journey of Discovery during the same month (May 17, 1673). We agreed that my eldest son, David, would accompany me on the first 24-mile leg, from Prairie du Sac to Spring Green. The decision to have David lead the trip was unrelated to birth order; it was mandated by lowly logistics. He graduated from college two weeks earlier and would be moving to New York City in mid-June to begin his professional career. Hence, just one brief window of time allowed him to share in the grand adventure.

Though more by happenstance than deliberate choice, it seemed a happy coincidence to begin the journey with David so soon after his graduation. He was beginning a dramatic and pivotal new phase of his life—being birthed from the cocoon of formal education into the "real world" experience. And like all births, it involved some dying to his (and my) old ways. Thus for me his graduation day resembled his biological birth, exciting but scary. Quite scary actually.

Oddly, none of the typical things concerned me: David's distance from home, capability in the marketplace, life in the big city, and other after-college challenges. Rather, my sense of panic came from memories that were awakened in prayer. Yes, prayer. The day before this momentous occasion, I tried to recall prayerfully, in as much vivid detail and active emotion as possible, all the blessed moments in my son's life. I was humbled and saddened by the haziness of my memories. The basic events were easy enough to catalog: birthdays, family vacations, academic milestones, and athletic accomplishments, but the fullness of the experience seemed like vapor. I could vaguely recall the misty form of the events, but not so much the substantial reality—conversations, laughter, food, and feelings—of those blessed days.

Thank God for the power of photographs! Old photo albums helped guide my memory and meditation so that I could envision the events. As I looked at those faded colors of youthful faces, a vibrant thankfulness suddenly pumped within my heart. As the details came back, I was overcome by a loving ache—that substantial, concrete, forceful, bursting of love—that was awakened and drawn forth from deep within me.

And that was enough. It was good. It was powerful. And then, I was at peace. Sure, I still had regrets. Regret that I had not been as loving and self-giving to my son as I would have desired. Regret that I had not appreciated the joy of all those moments with the type of attention that such exquisite experiences of love should receive. But still, I felt peace…and resolve. Resolve to love my son better, fuller, heartier in the telescoped days to come.

In light of this profound prayer experience, it seemed *apropos* to begin our canoe journey on Memorial Day, as it was a weekend on which we celebrated a rather fortuitous blending of the secular and the sacred. On the secular side, the weekend is consecrated for remembering those who have sacrificed their lives for us. And liturgically, it is the Feast of the Body and Blood of Christ, a time to recollect the gift of the Eucharist made possible by Jesus' sacrifice. Like the photo albums of my family that reawakened a loving ache within me, the Eucharist helps us to contextualize God's presence in our hectic lives and to become aware that every moment is a gift from God.

A Banquet Beginning

Jacques Marquette started his river journey with the Eucharist. Louis Jolliet, the coleader of the expedition, arrived at Marquette's mission church at Saint Ignace on the shores of Lake Superior on the Feast of the Immaculate Conception (December 8, 1672). Jolliet bore good news: the French governor had commissioned Jolliet, and the Jesuit superiors had given permission to Marquette to seek a fabled great river to the west which, according to Native American legends, emptied into the salty sea.

This dream adventure did not appear from thin air for Jolliet and Marquette. The two young men had worked earnestly for this authorization for years. They had studiously planned and prepared for such an adventure. Marquette, who had a facility with languages, had studied the Illinois tongue from a brave who had wandered north, far from his homeland along the banks of the Mississippi in the state now named after this tribe. Marquette and Jolliet had started to draw a rudimentary map of the rivers from Lake Michigan to the Mississippi, based on the information gleaned from the far-ranging Illinois nation and members of the tribes in the Great Lakes region—Winnebago, Menominee, Ojibwa, Ottawa, Fox, and Sauk—who had been daring enough to wander past their tribal territories into the Lakota (Sioux) lands that lay between them and the Great River.

Their dream was about to become a reality. Marquette's diary, which he wrote during this historic trip, recounts this auspicious moment with these words:

> The Feast of the Immaculate Conception of the Blessed Virgin—whom I have always invoked since I have been in this country of the Ottawas, to obtain from God the grace of being able to visit the nations who dwell along the Mississippi River—was precisely the day on which Monsieur Jolliet arrived with orders from Count Frontenac, our governor, and Monsieur Talon, our intendant, to accomplish this discovery with me. I was all the more delighted by this good news, since I saw that my plans were about to be accomplished, and since I found myself in the blessed necessity of exposing my life for the salvation of all these peoples, and especially for the Illinois, who had very urgently entreated me, when I was at Point St. Esprit, to carry the word of God to their country. (Marquette, *Jesuit Relations [JR]*, 189)

Thus we can well imagine that Marquette celebrated the Mass of the Feast of the Immaculate Conception that day with a particular sense of gratitude. The appropriateness of the feast was not lost on him. An idea for which he and Jolliet had long prepared was now being conceived so that their dream could be incarnated and born in the near future—that summer!

While Marquette was motivated by missionary zeal, the French government had economic motives. They hoped that the Mississippi emptied into the Pacific Ocean. If it did, then Columbus' long-ago dream of finding a water route to the Orient would finally be realized. Furthermore, Jolliet was to claim all newly explored lands for France. Their journey, in fact, resulted in the French laying claim to the very heartland of America—the broad swath of land from the Ohio Valley to the Rocky Mountains. The last vast section of this land—more than 800,000 square miles—shifted to American hands when President Thomas Jefferson signed the Louisiana Purchase with Napoleon Bonaparte in 1803.

After celebrating Mass, Marquette's first step toward exploration of the unknown waters was extensive preparation—for he was soon to enter totally foreign territory. On a decidedly different yet comparable level, the first step in one's individual spiritual journey can feel just as foreign. According to the *Spiritual Exercises* by Saint Ignatius Loyola (founder of Marquette's Jesuit order), the first step in the spiritual journey is to enter the River of Life by allowing the power of memory to situate us within the first God Question: *What is our place in the world?* What bubbles up is not an answer, but an experience: gratitude. By the contractions of memory, the first God Question, if authentically asked and lived in, births us into gratitude for all that God has given us. But the work of the first God Question is not done. It has more shaping, pushing, and emerging to do.

Short Paddles

The paddles are too short. The Epiphany paddles...they are the wrong size. That's what my oldest son David discovers as we frantically pack the car for the first leg of the journey. If you look at the paddles on their own, they appear sufficient. But now, as my son stands with his paddle next to our borrowed canoe, the discrepancy becomes obvious. David needs a bigger paddle.

As crises go, this one is easily solved. We just need to go to the store on our way to the river and buy a longer paddle. But the mistake bothers me. Is this a "sign" that my ability to prepare my sons for their adult lives has also fallen short? Or was it simply that my sons are now more men than the children of my memories? Either way, it bothers me.

In any case, the paddle issue adds to our packing problems

because we are behind schedule. I returned—late—from an out-of-town Memorial Day weekend soccer tournament with my youngest son. David and I need to get to the river before the canoe shuttle company closes for the day, so that we can make arrangements to have our car driven to our takeout location at the end of our three-day, two-night trip. I dash around the house and garage, madly grabbing sleeping bags, cooking supplies, and the tent. That tent! It is an inauspicious start for a journey that I have long held in my dreams.

We speed across the Wisconsin highway to Prairie du Sac, a town in the middle of the state and the starting point for this four-legged journey. Father Jacques Marquette actually entered the Wisconsin River by the city of Portage, which is a little farther upstream. But a dam (the last one on the river) located just north of Prairie du Sac prevents us from precisely reenacting that part of Marquette's trip.

Anxiously, we pull into the shuttle service's parking lot, hoping that they have not yet closed. The company's main business is renting canoes to people for day-trips down the river. "You're lucky," says the woman who greets us. "We've got one last group that arrived late at the pickup point. Otherwise, we'd be closed by now. They just called me from their cell phone. By the sounds of it, they've been doing more beer drinking than canoe paddling!" The company had a busy weekend. "Seeing as this is Memorial Day, you're leaving on a good day," she continued. "Now that the long weekend is over, hardly anyone is on the river. Plus, the wind will push you right along from the back. The wind usually comes from the west, right in your face. The wind blows from the east only about four or five days each summer. You'll make good time." Things are looking up! I decide to interpret the open river and favorable wind as the *real* omen for this trip.

After loading our canoe, I take the stern seat while David sits in the front. We shove off into the cool, inviting water. Finally we have begun the journey! I yell up toward David something about being on the same river that led Jacques Marquette to his great discovery. Like Marquette before us, our arms dip the paddles in the water to pull us forward. With an odd sense of reliving an ancient moment, we see the same dense shoreline and expansive sky as our mentors. Like them, our conversation is full of talk about adventure and discovery. With them, our hearts are full of gratitude for this gift of God called life.

After arduously paddling upstream from Green Bay, Marquette and his companions stopped by a Menominee village, where previous Jesuit missionaries had preached. Marquette reports in his diary a somewhat unsettling interaction with the tribe members:

> I told these Wild Rice People of my design to go and dis- cover remote nations in order to teach them the myster- ies of our holy religion. They were greatly surprised and did their best to dissuade me. They told me that I would meet nations who never show mercy to strangers, but break their heads for no reason, and that war was raging among various peoples who dwelt upon our route, which exposed us to the further manifest danger of being killed by the bands of warriors in their campaigns. They also said that the great river was very dangerous when one does not know the difficult passages, that it was full of horrible monsters who devoured men and canoes together, that there was even a demon who was heard from a great distance and who barred the way, swallowing up all who ventured to approach him, and finally that the heat was so excessive in those countries that it would inevitably cause our death.
>
> I thanked them for the good advice they gave me but told them that I could not follow it because the salvation

of souls was at stake, for which I would be delighted to give my life; that I scoffed at the alleged demon; that we would easily defend ourselves against those sea monsters; and, moreover, that we would be on our guard to avoid the other dangers with which they threatened us. After leading them in a prayer to God and giving them some instruction, I separated from them. (*JR*, 191)

Vicious warriors. Dangerous waters. Demon snakes. Oppressive heat. None of these obstacles dissuaded Marquette. But his fear was certainly raised when they came to the Mascouten village on the Fox River, thirty leagues from the portage path that would take them to the Wisconsin River. Upon arriving at this village, Marquette wrote that he was

greatly consoled by the sight of a handsome cross erected in the middle of the town and adorned with many white skins, red belts, and bows and arrows which these good people had offered to the great Manitou (this is the name which they give to God). They did this to thank him for having pity on them during the winter and for giving them an abundance of game when they most dreaded famine. (*JR*, 194)

But this consolation to Marquette's spirit was short-lived. They too feared venturing into the territory of the Lakota. The Mascouten offered the services of two guides to show them the portage to the Wisconsin River, but they refused to journey beyond that point.

The guides led them through the labyrinth of swamps and backwaters until they came to the portage trail, which Marquette measured as 2,700 paces. After helping them transport their supplies and two canoes, the guides departed. Now alone on the cusp of an alien land, Marquette then led the little band in a prayer to the Blessed Virgin of the Immaculate Conception, a prayer they recited every morning, before they once again set off during the expedition.

Marquette then cryptically reports, "after encouraging one another, we entered our canoes." But maybe one of his biographers got the scene right:

> When the two helpful Maumee guides disappeared down the barely perceptible portage trail on their way back to the Mascouten village, the seven venturesome Frenchmen finally severed the last tenuous ties with lands and people in any manner familiar to them. The profound sense of utter separation from the world they knew and their complete dependence on heavenly aid during their excursion into the unknown shine forth clearly in Marquette's entry in his journal on that occasion....

> With very little effort of the imagination one can picture those seven Frenchmen grouped hesitantly on the banks of the Wisconsin, looking a little fearfully downstream. Where did this new river really go? Was there, by chance, any substance to the Indian tales of monsters and giant whirlpools, dangers they could not hope to evade? Were they being foolhardy to go on? This was *Ultima Thule*, the end of the known world. Why go farther and for what purpose? (Donnelly, *Jacques Marquette, S.J.*, 212–213)

With only questions to lead them, they went into the great unknown, trusting the Mystery.

The woman at the canoe rental company is right; we fly down the river! The sun is warm, the breeze is refreshing, and the water is brilliant. And David is a strong paddler. But that is no surprise. He has always been a person of determination who sets high goals for himself.

I remember walking into his room once when he was a freshman in high school and seeing that he had tacked a sheet of paper onto the ceiling above his bed. When I asked him, "What's that?" He replied, "My top five life goals." Mystified by the location, I inquired, "Why did you put that list up there?" He replied, "So that the first thing I see in the morning and the last thing at night are the goals that I want to accomplish."

Curious, I looked up and chuckled as I read the first goal: "Make First Team All-American in Volleyball." My amused response was not trying to be cruel, just realistic. Despite a strong tradition of boys' volleyball in Milwaukee—and, at the club level, it is serious and competitive—the California beaches are the recruiting grounds for most volleyball talent. Besides this geographic hindrance, David's height made such a goal rather a (literal) stretch—even as an adult today, David is only about 5' 9" tall. In competitive volleyball, height is a real asset since it greatly enhances blocking and hitting the ball over the net. Once in high school, a male player better be at least 6' tall; most are in the 6' 3" to 6' 8" range.

But a fire burned in David's belly. He spent hours in the back-yard refining his athletic skills and he was fortunate enough to have some very talented teammates. So this diminutive setter (the "short" guy who bumps the ball up to be spiked by the giants) led his club team to successive invitations to the national tournament. The cold-weather Milwaukee team consistently beat the warm-weather powerhouses from California and Hawaii. When he was sixteen years old, his team made it to the national championship game. Unfortunately, they lost, but second in the nation was a phenomenal accomplishment. That year, David was named First Team All-American. My son had gotten the last laugh. Ah, the power of living an intentional life!

Landmarks on the shore speed by as we paddle efficiently down the river, and our progress reflects my own regret about the swiftness of time. He's growing up so very quickly....He's leaving home so soon....Time's moving too fast....Rushing right by....Almost gone....Past. "I'm not ready for him to go," I think as I look at his straining back as we paddle forward.

My concerns about David must have paled in comparison to those felt by Jacques Marquette's parents. Part of the French aristocracy, the Marquette family was not supportive when Jacques joined the Jesuits at the age of seventeen. His vocation, they thought, would squander the privileges that they carefully cultivated for him since his birth in 1637. They groomed him to achieve an expansive life defined by glory, fame, and honor in the halls of power and prestige. Joining the Jesuits? To them, their son was choosing a constricted life, the path to insignificance and unimportance. By their standards, Jacques was not choosing new life, but deserting.

How terribly horrified they must have been when they learned in 1666 that their son had been assigned by his Jesuit superiors to leave France and go to the New World. For Jacques this was the fulfillment of his childhood dream: to become a missionary in a foreign land. For his parents, it must have been a nightmare. It is one thing to have your child choose a different career path, but quite another to watch helplessly as the path leads to the fledgling Indian missions around Lake Superior. Given the difficulty of sea voyages in the seventeenth century, they certainly had to expect that he would never recross the ocean to return to France. In all likelihood, they would never see their son again. In fact, this premonition proved true; Marquette died in 1675 on the shores of Lake Michigan. He was just shy of 38 years of age.

I don't know if Marquette tacked his childhood goals—with "Become a foreign missionary" heading the list—above his bed. But I do know that, as a young man in the Jesuits, a spiritual principle was ingrained within his soul. It was the First Principle and Foundation of Ignatius' *Spiritual Exercises*:

> Human persons are created to praise, reverence, and serve God our Lord, and by this means [encounter the soul's salvation]. The other things on the face of the earth are

created for us, to help us in attaining the purpose for which we are created. Therefore, we are to make use of them insofar as they help us attain our purpose, and we should rid ourselves of them insofar as they hinder us from attaining it. Thus we should make ourselves indifferent to all created things, insofar as we are allowed free choice and are not under any prohibition. Consequently, as far as we are concerned, we should not prefer health to sickness, riches to poverty, honor to dishonor, a long life to a short life. The same holds for all other things. Our one desire and choice should be what will best help us attain the purpose for which we are created. (Elisabeth Meier Tetlow, trans., *The Spiritual Exercises of Saint Ignatius of Loyola*, 11)

The First Principle and Foundation maps our course; it places us on God's river of love. However, it does not provide answers, and it is not a goal. All it does is orient us, like a compass. Ignatius properly named this fundamental orientation the *First* Principle and Foundation. If a house's foundation is not properly laid, then the structure that rests on it will, at best, be misshapen and always vulnerable to collapse. Likewise, we must order our lives on this proper spiritual foundation. Only then will we find harmony in the midst of the tensions of life.

In order to live a life that praises, reverences, and serves God, Ignatius asserts that we must approach life with a challenging type of freedom, which he calls indifference. *Indifference* is a hard word. It is easy to misunderstand and difficult to do. The misunderstanding stems from our modern use of the term *indifference*, which typically means apathy, insensitivity, or unconcern. This is not the meaning that Ignatius has in mind when he uses the word. For this reason, the Jesuit, David Fleming, suggests translating *indifference* as "in balance." This translation is not a bad explanation of indifference, but even so, *balance* does not uncover Ignatius' deeper point when he uses the term *indifference*.

Instead, for Ignatius indifference was another way of talking about the dynamics of love. That's right, love. For if we truly believe that God's loving presence is in all created things, including us, then this must mean that nothing can separate us from that love. So one reason Ignatius demands that we not desire health over sickness, riches over poverty, honor over dishonor, a long life over a short life, and so forth is because we should desire a relationship with God—with the One who, as Saint Francis of Assisi eloquently proved, exists and persists in "lesser" things. This is *not* to say that God wants us to be sick or die prematurely, but rather that all things provide opportunities for moments of grace, and so we can experience God even in the "negative" moments of life.

Another aspect of indifference reveals the "tricky" thing about love: it is only possible to love if we are free. We know this from our human love relationships. When bound by our self-interest or our self-delusion, our ability to love another person is limited because we cannot really give ourselves to the other person. And love is, at its very root, all about self-giving. Since I can only give myself to the degree that I am free, this *de facto* implies that I can only love to the degree that I am free. The circle of love can only be entered through the portal of freedom. Indifference cultivates within us a radical form of freedom from our self-interest so that we are capable of loving God to the greatest degree possible. *That* is a challenge!

Notice that indifference always creates tension for us because our choice of action is not predetermined. Ignatius does not privilege wealth over poverty or poverty over wealth. Instead, we are to desire whatever brings us closer to God. Joseph Tetlow put it this way:

> So whether I find a thing attractive or not, I will choose only those things that lead me to God and toward my most authentic self. This seems obvious and simple, but consider what it entails: I will not have a fixed determi-

nation always to choose one alternative over others.... No. I will hold myself in balance until I have decided which concrete alternative will lead me to God and to loving those around me. (Tetlow, *Choosing Christ in the World,* 172)

In other words, we are simply put on the river, loving the moment and the movement in and of itself.

This is why the First Principle and Foundation is not a goal; rather, it is a way of placing ourselves in relationship. Goals can be very good. They can give us direction and a sense of accomplishment. But goals point to the future, not the present. Goals are about who we want to be, not about how God has made us. Goals entail a certain limitation, a certain narrowness, a certain constriction. They are hard and fast. They orient us not in relation to who we are, but who we are not. They put us on the solid shore of concrete tasks, not in the flowing river of responsive love.

We Americans are somewhat spiritually handicapped because our culture mistakenly and continually tells us that we are nothing until we have accomplished our goals. Our culture screams that the future is *the* thing, the only important thing that matters. And that's the problem. Goals point us to things, but life is about living in a relationship. Life is about being in the river, not about getting to the shore.

So the first God Question—*What is our place in the world?*— is about seeing that God has placed us personally and profoundly in a web of divine love. All of life is a gift from a loving God who desires only to enter into a loving relationship with us. But love requires freedom. So we must find the place of *indifference* to appreciate that God is radically found in all things so that all things are ultimately means to know and love God. The first God Question is about truly living in Ignatius' First Principle and Foundation. Stated metaphorically, it is about placing us in the river. It is about reminding us that all of Creation, and we, as well, are always and forever in the birth channel of God's very womb.

Beach Walkers

Paddling aggressively to make up for our late start makes it hard to have any in-depth conversation. About eight miles downriver, I yell to David, "Let's hug the north side of the river for a little bit." "Why's that?" asks David. I stammer and stall, and then I see David smile when I finally come out with it. "Well, according to the river map, we are approaching a 'clothing optional' stretch of beach on the south side." This does not really cause any problems, as the Wisconsin is a broad river, extending to a half-mile width in places. While it is probably less than that at this point, it is still sufficient to avoid any embarrassing contact with nudists. Besides, it is early evening. So, even though the long summer sun is still warm, surely most of the "birthday suit" bathers have headed home.

As we come closer to the beach, we see on the distant shore a departing couple walking up the beach toward us. I see David glance over at them, look again, remove his gaze, then return to stare intently. Bemused, it is now my turn to smile because I am guessing that David is trying to figure out if this couple is wearing bathing suits. You can tell that one is a man and the other is a woman, but the clothing issue is a mystery given the distance. Approaching the very east edge of the strip of beach, the couple stops, pulls some things out of their bag, and it becomes clear that they are donning bathing suits. Mystery solved!

Or is it? Is it just accidental that right at the beginning of the Bible (see Genesis 2) we stumble across two people who are emphatically described as living in a "clothing optional" Garden? There it is, boldly proclaimed: "And the man and his wife were both naked, and were not ashamed" (2:25). Now, as a biblical scholar, I know the rational explanation for this odd narrative detail. Genesis has an affinity for etiological tales, which is just a fancy name for stories about the source or origin of things. So, the ancients wondered, why are humans the only animals to wear clothes? The Genesis story provides an explanation: God made them for us when we were expelled from the Garden.

I wonder if there isn't something deeper, something more unconscious, more mysterious, more potent at play here in Genesis. After all, this is the foundational story about the human-divine relationship. Maybe the narrative's remark about two naked people points us to some important dynamic about how we are placed within God's presence. In this regard, the biblical verse directly before this "naked" stuff is revealing: "Therefore a man leaves his father and his mother and clings to his wife, and they become one flesh" (Genesis 2:24). There it is: God made us so that our very *desire* for each other moves us *toward* each other, toward unity. And since God works with us in the way he made us, then God also works through our desires to draw us to God's own self. As the end of the Garden story makes it clear, our human desires, not just sexual ones, but *all* our desires, either draw us into or away from relationship with each other and with God.

It's shocking to say that the human experience of longing, which is so profoundly present in the desire of a man for a woman, and a woman for a man, is also an experience of God drawing us to his very self. Saint Augustine was basically saying the same thing when he said, "Our desire is our prayer." Can someone put some clothes on that thought!

Clothing (covering) our desires covers up the questions, and it is only through questions that we can faithfully unpack this insight's significance. *Seeking* or *desiring* or *longing* is indeed the first step to falling in love with God. But while seeking is essential, it is incomplete. Like any kind of romantic love, in its unchanneled state it more readily awakens us to our incompleteness than to our wholeness. That is what happened in the Garden story: Adam and Eve are roused to their desire for wholeness (that is, knowledge of all things) by the snake.

We, as humans, intuitively know that we are incomplete as individuals. The psychologist Erich Fromm teaches us that humans are from the moment of their birth shaped by an innate and

unshakable experience of separateness, isolation, and alienation—
and that throughout our lives we are psychologically driven to
seek unity, at-one-ness, and fullness (Fromm, *Man for Himself,*
54–55). Saint Thomas Aquinas teaches roughly the same thing
when he said that our human nature has an "appetite for completion" (*Summa Theologica* II, 1.6). Our desires make us aware of
this foreboding sense of isolation and deep longing for connection
to something greater than ourselves. Because of desire, we come
to realize that we are intractably drawn to another because of
our longing for wholeness. This *desire*, this *longing*, this *seeking*
is what initially draws us to each other and ultimately to God
because it lays bare an embarrassing fact: we are not enough, we
are not complete, we are not whole. No matter how many goals
we achieve, we cannot escape this truth.

If this search for God stops at seeking, it is a shallow and
superficial vision of God's goodness and love. That's what happened in the Garden: this desire for wholeness was misordered
when Adam and Eve sought completion by eating the fruit of the
Tree of the Knowledge of Good and Evil. Nevertheless, our first
task is indeed to seek to *know* God. Intriguingly, the Hebrew
word for "know" *(yada´)* in the Old Testament indicates not so
much an act of the intellect, but rather means coming to know
something through experience or familiarity, a willing adhesion
of the "person knowing" to what is "known," an immersion into
the sought reality. In fact, *yada´* is often used in the Bible as a
euphemism for having intimate sexual relations, but it generally
refers to a "relationship." It is only when we know God in this
manner—through relationship—that we can truly love God.

Asserting that our fundamental impulse toward God is to be
found in and through our desires, even in sexual desires, might
sound radical and even verging on heresy. But if it is, then Pope
Benedict XVI is in hot water, too. In his first encyclical, God Is
Love (*Deus Caritas Est),* he argues that *eros*—the Greek word for
desire, especially sexual desire—is a divine gift that is the starting
point for love and thus central in our relationship with God. God,

says Pope Benedict, *is* love according to the First Letter of John. Benedict also sees the story of Adam and Eve as pointing us to the fundamental role of desire in the spiritual life:

> Now Adam finds the helper that he needed: "This at last is bone of my bones and flesh of my flesh" (*Gen* 2:23)....The idea is certainly present that man is somehow incomplete, driven by nature to seek in another the part that can make him whole, the idea that only in communion with the opposite sex can he become "complete". The biblical account thus concludes with a prophecy about Adam: "Therefore a man leaves his father and his mother and cleaves to his wife and they become one flesh" (*Gen* 2:24).
>
> Two aspects of this are important. First, *eros* is somehow rooted in man's very nature; Adam is a seeker, who "abandons his mother and father" in order to find woman; only together do the two represent complete humanity and become "one flesh". The second aspect is equally important. From the standpoint of creation, *eros* directs man towards marriage, to a bond which is unique and definitive; thus, and only thus, does it fulfill its deepest purpose. (*DCE* 11)

Benedict further claims that this marital union between man and woman "becomes the icon of the relationship between God and his people and vice versa" (*DCE* 11). Like Saint Augustine, Saint Francis de Sales, and many other spiritual masters, Benedict sees love as inescapably beginning with desire, and only then capable of moving to *agape*, the Greek word for selfless or sacrificial love. But that is not Benedict's biggest bombshell, for then he writes: "God's way of loving becomes the measure of human love" (*DCE* 11). Based on this principle, Benedict comes to a stunning conclusion: God's love also begins with *eros*, with desire—desire for relationship with his creation... and particularly with us.

According to theologian Ulrich Lehner, August Adam, whose 1931 book *The Primacy of Love* influenced Benedict's *Deus Caritas Est*, articulated the connection between passion and love in this manner: "Eros is not only a demonic power, which destroys, ruins, and captivates all life. It is also a source of energy, which is able to overcome the world. The love between man and woman, which the Creator put in their hearts as one of the mightiest desires...is also one of the greatest power sources of human culture" (Adam, *The Primacy of Love*, as cited in Lehner, "Improper Wisdom," 16). Desire is thus mutually terrifying and magnificent: a potent gift!

This same insight lies at the very heart of Saint Ignatius' *Spiritual Exercises*. The *Exercises* are, ultimately, all about falling in love with God. As we all know, the first step in falling in love is desire: the desire for the other. Desire is at the core of human experience. Desires are somewhat mysterious; their power can both elate and frighten us. Part of their power is that they can lead us to unexpected places; they take us beyond ourselves. Thus, we experience our desires as a mysterious and transcendent force. Mysterious and transcendent force...not a bad definition of God!

For Ignatius, our desires, if properly discerned, ordered, and responded to, are the primary way that God speaks to us. God has ordered us so that our fundamental human desires are to seek completeness, wholeness, and happiness. As we allow this process to unfold in our lives, we discover God's will. Not surprisingly, completeness, wholeness, and happiness are God's synonyms for another word: *love*. And, as the First Letter of John reminds us, "God is love, and those who abide in love abide in God, and God abides in them" (4:16). So if our primary desire is love—and God is love—then we are being drawn back to God. Hence, our most basic desire as human beings is a desire for God.

If we return to the first God Question, we realize that we are made, and thus placed, as passion (loving) people. Asking "what are my desires?" is just another way of asking the first God Question. God places us through our desires, but they must be properly ordered to the First Principle and Foundation: toward the purpose for which we were made. We must realize that purpose is not a goal, but our nature; it is not an answer, but a question that continually redefines us.

Bluff Viewing

We missed it. It must have been somewhere back upstream. But our unrefined city eyes had not picked up the subtle break in the dense forest line. The beach "distraction" hadn't helped either. We had lost our place on the river—and thus our focus on what we were seeking.

So now we have turned around, straining against our paddles, fighting the strong current. "Is that it?" I shout to David. "I think so," he responds. "It looks like a trail." As we approach the shore, we know we've found the right spot: the landing for Ferry Bluff. We hop out of the canoe, pull it ashore, and tie the bowline to a nearby tree. We begin hiking up the trail to the top of the bluff.

It is about a mile trek to the summit of Ferry Bluff, one of the taller peaks along the Wisconsin River. It is a steep climb, but it feels good to stretch our legs. We arrive at the top out of breath, brought on by the ascent and the breathtaking view. The land to the south consists of a gently rising plain, while the north bank is studded by jutting bluffs covered with trees except for their sheer rocky faces. From this vantage point, the river appears cradled within a massive green hand. The palm's features emerge from the rolling carpet of trees to the south, and the stout, flat-topped northern hills appear as the curling fingers that gently press the serpentine river as if to hold it in its course. The amazing vista leaves one astonished by the splendor of creation.

Maybe it was a similar experience that inspired the nineteenth-century Jesuit Gerard Manley Hopkins to pen his poem, "God's Grandeur."

> *The world is charged with the grandeur of God.*
> *It will flame out, like shining from shook foil;*
> *It gathers to a greatness, like the ooze of oil.*
> *Crushed. Why do men then now not reck his rod?*
> *Generations have trod, have trod, have trod;*
> *And all is seared with trade; bleared,*
> *smeared with toil;*
> *And wears man's smudge and shares man's smell:*
> *the soil*
> *Is bare now, nor can foot feel, being shod.*
>
> *And for all this, nature is never spent;*
> *There lives the dearest freshness deep down things;*
> *And though the last lights off the black West went*
> *Oh, morning, at the brown brink eastward,*
> *springs—*
> *Because the Holy Ghost over the bent*
> *World broods with warm breast and with ah!*
> *Bright wings.*

The panoramic view is indeed charged with God's grandeur, but the informational placards around the observation point (courtesy of the Wisconsin Department of Natural Resources) are bleak reminders of humanity's smear. One sign explains that the bluff's name comes from the Civil War years when a man named Moses Laws (not to be confused with the Law of Moses) operated a ferry here. For fifteen years, Laws used poles to pull the ferry loaded with human passengers, nervous livestock, and farm wagons. Back and forth across the river, he labored daily over the surface of this river, an obstacle he overcame again and again. But I wonder if he ever truly entered the river, allowing its depths to carry him, move him, journey him. His trodding toil ended ignominiously. One day he stumbled and unluckily fell on the spout of an oil can that stabbed him through the eye, killing him instantly. *"All is seared with trade,"* said Hopkins, and the ferryman was living (and dead) proof of the proliferation of commerce on the river.

Another informational sign tells the story of the "river hogs," the most dangerous job in the lumber business, which was Wisconsin's leading industry during the nineteenth century. Lumberjacks spent the winter harvesting trees and binding them into cribs beside the river. When the spring thaw turned the Wisconsin River into a swollen, rushing freeway, the trees were shoved into the river, bound for St. Louis and other sawmills along the Mississippi. The river hogs rode on the semi-truck–sized cribs like jockeys, dangerously balancing atop these half-frozen torpedoes as they desperately steered them down the roiling river and over treacherous rapids. Many drowned when they were cast into the bone-chilling waters or were maimed as limbs were severed between the slamming logs.

But logjams were the most dangerous part of the job for the river hogs. The river was so forceful that logs would pile up more than twenty feet above the level of the river. A river hog would then climb over the front of the logjam, find and pry loose the "key log," and then frantically scramble to avoid the crushing logs cascading around him. The body counts during these spring drives raised as high as these logjams...so high that the mill owners reportedly lost track of the number. Certainly, as with Hopkins, these heroic river hogs understood what it meant to be *"bleared, [and] smeared with toil."*

The history of humanity's striving futility on this river does not end there. The next informational sign describes Black Hawk's War. The gravity of the ominous term *war* masks this wretched tragedy. Citing the authority of some disputed treaties (the most notorious of which was negotiated by William Henry Harrison, who would later become the ninth president of the United States), in the summer of 1831 the U.S. Army forced Black Hawk's band to move from their tribal lands in southern Wisconsin and northern Illinois to the west side of the Mississippi—and ordered them never to return to their homelands. Humiliated by his treatment at the hands of the American military, angered by the U.S. government's shortchanging of his corn rations during the previous winter, bolstered by spurious British promises of military support, and heartened by the invitation of White Cloud, a Winnebago prophet, to come live in his federally protected village in northern Illinois, Black Hawk and his tribe decided to recross the Mississippi in the spring of 1832.

The Anglo population panicked. The regional Superintendent of Indian Affairs located in St. Louis, William Clark of "Lewis and Clark," was alarmed. Federal troops, some led by another future president, Colonel Zachary Taylor, arrived via steamboat from St. Louis. Four thousand Illinois militia men, including a twenty-three-year-old captain named Abraham Lincoln, were mustered. Black Hawk soon realized that the British were not coming and that he was putting his Winnebago hosts in harm's way. He decided that the current of white anger was too strong and that he would return peacefully to the west side of the Mississippi.

As so often is the case in American history, though, fear trumps peace. Black Hawk's representatives, walking under a white flag, were killed by Illinois militia men who did not understand the Sauk tongue. The Black Hawk "War" had begun. Black Hawk moved north, ultimately reaching the Wisconsin River. Facing a military force that was at times almost ten times larger than his own, Black Hawk and his five hundred warriors engaged in a series of pitched rearguard battles along the river's banks as they furiously strove to protect their women, children, and elderly. The band's retreat was continually cut off by the U.S. Army, but they bravely and ingeniously outmaneuvered the better-equipped troops, zigzagging in all directions along the river basin. After almost three months of fighting, hiding, and running, the starving remnant of the band finally made it to the banks of the Mississippi. But as they were recrossing to the Iowa side, a military gunboat intercepted them. Once again, the bearers of a white flag were killed. A massacre ensued. By the end of the protracted summer hostilities, almost all of the thousand members of Black Hawk's original band were killed. Their blood is soaked into the sands of the river's course. Hopkins reminds us that the river *"wears man's smudge and shares man's smell: the soil."*

Incongruously, Black Hawk himself escaped, although he later surrendered to the U.S. Army and was escorted to prison by a troop of soldiers commanded by Lieutenant Jefferson Davis, who would become the president of the Confederate States during the Civil War. So why did Black Hawk undertake such a foolhardy mission? His motives must have been mixed, but he once gave this uncomplicated reason: "I wish to remain where the bones of my fathers are laid." This feared warrior was actually sixty-five years old when he took that fateful step across the Mississippi. This old man—who might even be called ancient, given nineteenth-century life expectancy rates—was simply striving to find his place...his final place...in the world by laying his bones next to the bones of those who came before him. Maybe he took this imprudent, gasping journey because he knew deep down that our ultimate place is not defined by whether we become a diligent worker, a daring pioneer, or a great president, but by our position in proper connection with all that was and all that is. Unfortunately, Black Hawk's attempt to find that place was stifled by hot-fired hatred that hardened into clay-dry fear. *"The soil is bare now,"* says Hopkins, *"nor can foot feel, being shod."*

The informational placards are obviously meant to impress visitors with the stirring course of human history that has flowed along the banks of the Wisconsin River. As stories, they honor the values of persistence, courage, and security; but I am struck that each story is one of a people in a constant agitated state of transportation, of movement, of flight. I then chuckle to myself as I realize that I am no different. I recall my own frantic pace in just getting this trip together—not only the last-minute packing earlier this very day, but even that stormy-night errand to buy the too-short Epiphany paddles. But then, if you recall how we commonly tell the story of Epiphany, it is about the wandering Three Wise Men journeying to visit some fellow travelers, a weary family. We know their woeful story: exhausted yet expectant, there was no room in the inns of Bethlehem. The only lodging was among beasts of burden. Then, amid the squalor, a child is born. Jesus!

Their story is similar to our own everyday experience. We are a nation of perpetual travelers, commuters constantly journeying from one location to another: to work and home, school and store, recreation and entertainment. For many, this hurried life of perpetual commuting is exhausting. There seems to be no room in our hectic schedules to relax even for a moment; nor is there time to relish fully the wonders of life, such as the love of family and the companionship of friends. Even like the Holy Family on that fateful night, we too lodge with our modern beasts of burdens (our cars), which we park inside our homes in our attached garages.

Finally, like those weary travelers long ago, we also hold within us a growing sense of expectation. This deep, unceasing urge within us drives us to search for some place of comfort and completeness in our lives. In a way, it is a holy restlessness, although it can also lead us to an even more frantic pace of life as we are bluffed into thinking that we can find meaning in things and activities that cannot grant rest to the true yearnings of the soul.

Because the constant, frantic twirling makes us dizzy, we confuse the edges of our lives with its essence and too quickly claim the superficial as substance. We Americans truly are what Richard Rohr calls "circumference people": people who live on the boundaries of our own lives, not at our center (*Everything Belongs*, 15–16). Hence, maybe it is no big surprise that when we hear Christmas Day's good news—"God has become human!"—

we stay stuck on the outer edges of this profound message and get the Incarnation's meaning all backwards. We mistakenly think that God has become human so that we can cast off our humanness. As a result, we worship God's journey to and from earth instead of *doing* Jesus' journey upon the earth.

Jesus' journey was to become human, and the purpose of his teachings and actions was to lead us to live authentic human lives. This must likewise be the journey we undertake: to become fully human. The irony—the paradox—is that by going to the center of our humanness, we enter into the mystery of God.

God knows of our difficulties with relationships. Maybe this is why God, who could have chosen to be born into an influential, royal family or in a powerful, wealthy country, came in the midst of a dirty, backwater town in Palestine. Only stories about unwelcome travelers, unpleasant stables, and unkempt cribs are enough to startle us into seeing the real message of Christmas: we do not know God except through, with, and in our imperfect, clumsy humanity.

Maybe at some deep, unconscious level we fear this message (even if we understand it) and thus we quickly cast off Christmas. Liturgically, Christmas lasts for twelve days, all the way to Epiphany. But in North America it ends shortly after it begins. By noon on December 25, radio stations stop playing Christmas carols. Less than twenty-four hours later, overstocked (and outdated) Christmas items are relegated to the bargain shelves, and withered Christmas trees, which have been standing since Thanksgiving, dot city curbs. Certainly by December 28, we are back to searing trade, smearing toil, and barren soil. Maybe we end Christmas so quickly because we would rather live in its benign memory than its blinding light. For this light does not lead us away from our humanness, but into it. The first God Question challenges us to encounter our place in the world. It reminds us that we must not try through the shear force of our spinning movement to fling off our humanity. Rather, we must enter it fully and authentically so that we might come into the presence of God.

River Forms

The first God Question leads us to further questions. How do I really enter into the heart of what it means to be human? Some method of circumspection is needed to avoid confusing our circumference (our external appearance) with our center (the core of our being). The next step is seeing the pattern of our lives as part of a larger story. It seems we need to continually put (or place) our lives within the larger context of God's creative action.

Our hilltop vista of the River Rendezvous offers just such a perspective. Here there is a fourth sign, a plaque describing two versions of the origins of the Wisconsin River, one scientific and the other mythic. The scientists tell us that the river's course was determined by the final massive glacier from the Ice Age, which stopped pretty much at the place in the river where we put in our canoe earlier in the afternoon. About 25,000 years ago, the last of the glaciers ground to a halt around the Wisconsin Dells, not far from some of the oldest rock outcroppings in North America: the durable and immovable Baraboo Hills. Accordingly, the resulting countryside (our path to the Mississippi) is known as the "Driftless Area" because the glaciers never "drifted" into this region. Spared the grinding pressure of the glacier, the region developed a unique topology.

As the earth's slow-warming atmosphere melted the colossal glacier into the resolute rock barrier of the Baraboo Hills, a huge lake was formed north of its stopping point. Although the solid Precambrian quartzite lime landscape could resist hard-moving ice, it was no match for soft-flowing water. Much like those river logjams of the nineteenth century, at some point the slow, unending movement of the water worked loose a keystone(s), and the waters of the glacial lake burst forth, weaving and cutting a deep river through the landscape as it fulfilled its gravitational commitment to the great waters of the ocean. It could do no other. It sought no other. It did no other. As Hopkins said, it *"Shook foil; It gathers to a greatness."*

That was about 10,000 years ago, an eternity for most of us who have trouble remembering our own childhood. However, scientists tell us that if we compare the earth's geological age to the average human lifespan, then the Wisconsin River was born just ninety minutes ago. This analogy of geological time to a human lifespan highlights another, even more profound ancient truth. Time measured in this fashion means that the combined lifetimes of the ferryman Moses Laws, the river hogs, Black Hawk, and the U.S. presidents who came to the area represent less than a minute in the earth's geological life. One brief moment in time!

Such brevity reminds us of our own temporal insignificance and our spiritual magnificence. Happily, we are not God, but only part of God's grand creation. As such, we are to see ourselves as the water, mysteriously powerful in our soft triviality. But it is because we are awash in something much more than ourselves—the Mystery—that our lives have endless meaning. Maybe Willa Cather expressed it best, when she wrote in her novel, *My Antonia,* "That is happiness; to be dissolved into something complete and great" (p. 18). Properly understood, the first God Question situates us within God's marvelous work, which is far greater than our mere existence.

The second version of the river's origins is told by a Native American myth. According to Winnebago legend, there once was a *manitou,* or spirit, who lived in the Northern Woods near the Big Lake (modern-day Lake Superior). One day he decided to leave for the sea. So the spirit took the form of a giant serpent and slithered southward, his great body carving a groove through the forest, which then filled with water. When he encountered rocks, he skimmed over them and even today the rushing waters in these places hiss like that snake. Then the snake came across a massive block of rock that he could not climb over. But he jammed his head into a crack. He pushed and strained until he burst through, leaving in his wake the twisted formations of the Wisconsin Dells.

After splitting the rock, the snake slid west, leaving behind the trail-tell sign of his S-slithering path. When the snake came to the Mississippi River, he swam upon it to the Great Waters (Atlantic Ocean). "...*Nature is never spent; There lives the dearest freshness deep down things*" (Hopkins, "God's Grandeur," 66).

What is it about snakes and water? They seem intrinsically related in the human subconscious. This association appears time and again in the mythological stories of the ancient Near East, the soil that nourished the faith of the Hebrew people and the literal location of a multitude of snakes. In these stories, snakes usually are portrayed both as the gods of water (good) and the forces of chaos and threat (evil).

The connection between water and evil snakes should not be glossed over too quickly. Unlike water, which is unconsciously driven by gravity and molecular nature to seek its source, we can misuse this divine gift through our actions, wreaking havoc in our lives and the world. God's gift entrusts us with a power so great that we can destroy God's desires for us. We can even obliterate millions of years of God's work upon the earth with the push of a button. What a colossal risk by God! And it all comes back to water. Even the hydrogen bomb—the ultimate icon of modern power—is made from one of the elements of water (H_2O). So water, like the mythic snake, is still a two-edged sword: the font of life and the power for destruction. This is why the first God Question is so important. It impels us to recognize that we must conform ourselves within the Mystery (the nourishing water of God's gift) so as not to abuse the fearful power that God has uniquely bestowed on us as his creatures.

In the end, the scientific and mythological versions of the birth of the Wisconsin River are not that different. Both are built on observations of the natural world. Both versions assume that some significant event happened in the Baraboo Hills that was directly related to the formation of a river. In one case, the eroding pressure of melted glacial ice created the river; in the other, the pushing head of a giant mythical snake. One version makes us aware of the humbling nature of time—we are just a blip in history. The other alerts us to the terrible aspects of freedom—we are powerful beyond measure.

Our study of the informational placards is interrupted by the arrival of a young couple hiking in the state park. I hear the same expressions of appreciation for the view as my son and I had upon our ascent. At the rocky edge of the bluff, they stand with their arms around each other and look at the stunning panorama. Then the young man points across the river and comments, "Hey, there's that nude beach!" (I told you it was infamous.) After a brief pause, he speaks in a voice clearly meant for more than his companion's ears, saying, "Standing on a bluff, looking at people in the buff!" Turning toward his girlfriend with a wry smile on his lips, his verbal cleverness is rewarded with a sharp elbow jabbed into his side (maybe where Adam's missing rib is located!). He feigns injury, and then re-embraces his main squeeze.

Bluff and buff. Very cute. And right on the mark. We need to see the majesty of the big picture, but most of us live our lives in our very chaotic skin. Life is ultimately about properly ordering our desires so that we can appropriately situate ourselves on this grand river of the life journey. Easy to see, hard to do.

Tent Fiasco

David and I walk down from the bluff and return to our canoe. Shoving off, we again paddle hard, trying to make it another mile downriver before we camp for the night. We find a great site with a broad southern-facing sandy beach.

We pull our canoe ashore and lug our gear about twenty yards from the shoreline. We have to set up fast; the evening light is fading and I want to start dinner before it is totally extinguished. We are still trying to make up for our rushed packing and late departure.

As David pulls the dome-style nylon tent from its bag, I say, "You know, I meant to swap the shorter stakes with longer ones. The longer ones work better in sand. But I only had time to grab this tent off the shelf and throw it in the car. But the wind seems to have died down, so I think we will be OK without them." Then, I hear David say, "Er, Dad, what is this?" I turn to see David holding a clump of nylon and a whole lot of wide white mesh. We unfold the mass of nylon to see a large snazzy logo printed in the middle along with these words, "World of Golf."

Instantly I say the inane: "Which of your brothers put the backyard golf net in the tent bag?" My sons gave me this golf net for my birthday the previous month. Just like a dome tent, it is held up by two intersecting bendable fiberglass poles and plastic stakes. But unlike a dome tent, it only consists of three sides of mesh netting, with a nylon "bull's-eye" attached to the middle panel. You hit real golf balls through the open side at that nylon square. In this way, you can, as the original box said, "Turn your backyard into a driving range." And what is really nifty is that it collapses to fit into a swell nylon bag…a bag that is about the same size and color as the bag for our dome tent. As I fume, the truth hits me like a ton of bricks…in my haste I grabbed the wrong bag off the shelf.

David, who still has a puzzled look on his face, asks, "Where's the real tent?" As I start to answer, I begin to laugh uncontrollably. Between gales, I can barely croak out, "At home." The absurdity of it all just releases itself in laughter. David too begins to shake with laughter. After literally rolling on the sand, we slowly regain our composure, until David sputters out, "Oh, Dad, this is terrible because I forgot to pack the sand wedge." More convulsive laughter, more rolling on the sand.

And it was great. Victor Borge once said that the shortest distance between two people is a good laugh. He is right. As David and I sit in the sand holding our golfing aid, I feel a bond, a grateful bond. And I promise myself: "Remember this. The fullness of it. The beauty of it. Don't let this moment drift into faded memory." But just to be sure, I take a picture of us holding up our evening shelter.

Using the golf net, its poles and stakes, plastic tarps, canoe paddles, and ropes, we jerry-rig a shelter. Luckily, there are no mosquitoes this early in the season; our concocted tent would have been useless in keeping them out, and totally ineffective in a storm. All it really does is keep the morning dew off us and provide some feeble sense of not being totally exposed to the night elements.

After making a fire, preparing our dinner, and talking late into the night, we crawl into our shelter. As I rethink over the day's events, I again start worrying about "omens." Does my packing of the wrong bag confirm that the short paddle that I bought for David signifies some failure on my part? Since he is about to leave home, maybe these are signs that I have failed as a father, that I have insufficiently armed him with a sense of place that will allow him to navigate life.

As I fret, I look up. The golf net's white mesh is large holed, so I have a clear view of the moonless night sky. It is brilliant! Staring up into that vast firmament, *it* comes upon me once again. (Maybe you, too, have had this experience.) It can happen almost any night that is clear, dark, and silent. We look up into the vault of stars, stretching beyond comprehension. Our heart seems to sink into the pit of our stomach as we realize our minuscule insignificance in this great expanse. Somehow the scientists' numbers—that our own little galaxy measures about 100,000 light-years across and each light-year is about 6 trillion miles—seem limp as a way of expressing the immensity of it all. Instead, consider that if we were able to shrink the entire universe into the Green Bay Packers' stadium, Lambeau Field, the earth would be the size of the head of a pin stuck into seat 23, row G... and thus we (humans) would be microscopic specks of dust on that pinhead! Unfortunately, these numbers numb us more than bear the mystery for us.

A foreboding sense of insignificance used to overwhelm and

almost swallow me in my fears. Then I learned that our very bodies are made up of stars. In fact, every material thing is nothing but stardust. As many scientists propose, every element in the universe is the byproduct of the big bang, that primal explosion that distributed matter into space and time. We Christians interpret the "bang" as a wondrous moment when God began his relationship with us. No new elements need to come into existence because no elements are destroyed or lost. Oh, sure, living things die and solid objects disintegrate, but the atomic elements are not lost. Rather, the creative universe—the ultimate conserver—re-forms and reconnects the elements to create a (re)new(ed) reality.

Once we accept our cosmic place in the world, we change our understanding of God's creative work in our lives. It frees us to reinterpret our place in the world. Maybe we, as humans, have known this subconsciously for ages. Maybe that is why the ancients, like those three Wise Men, often looked to the stars' movements to see if they could divine God's plan for them. Maybe that is why the English word *disaster* is the combination of two words ("dis" + "astrum"), which literally means "to be disconnected from the stars." And truly, such disconnection should be considered a disaster, for if we do not see ourselves as physically part of the cosmos (God's entire creation), then we do not know who we truly are because we do not really know our place. It is a spiritual disaster not to know that we are physically connected to that first creative spark of God.

This physical fact leads to a stunning realization: we are materially connected to every other person and all other living beings and substances in the world. In a very real way, every fat cell and every brain synapse, everything that we call "us," existed in some other form in some other human, creature, or substance before it became "us." Our bodies literally enflesh a dynamic history stretching back to the first moment in time, the first moment of Creation, the first action of God in this world. We truly are one with the universe, materially speaking.

But it goes further than that. We also must recognize that this tiny pinhead of a planet on which we stand is unique (as far as we know) in its creative ability. As Brian Swimme notes:

> We know of no other planet with Earth's creative power.... Earth created the land masses, the mountain ranges, the atmosphere. The moon and Mercury created mountain ranges but their creativity ended long ago. Mars, too, created mountains and a thick crust and an atmosphere, but its significant creative evolution has ceased....Only on Earth were the creative dynamics able to fashion such diversity, even on this elemental realm. Earth created the oceans, a stupendous feat. We have yet to find another ocean in this galaxy, another lake or river. We know of no others besides our own....We've found water vapor, and ice, but that is all....When we take the whole universe as our fundamental frame of reference, we begin to appreciate the cosmic significance of running water....
>
> Earth was a cauldron of chemical and elemental creativity, fashioning ever more complex forms and combinations until life burst forth in the oceans and spread across the continents, covering the entire planet. This creativity advanced until flowers bloomed on every continent, then advanced further until the vision of the flowers and all beauty could be deeply felt and appreciated. We are the latest, the most recent, the youngest extravagance of this stupendously creative Earth. (Swimme, *The Universe Is a Green Dragon*, 30–31)

And here is the real kicker: everything is inexorably drawn to something. Those star elements that make up all things in the universe are governed by a universal law of attraction that draws all things beyond themselves to seek unity or infusion. Ronald Rolheiser sees this physical principle as providing us with a profound spiritual insight:

God speaks to every element in the language it can understand. Thus, God lures hydrogen through its attraction to oxygen. God draws everything else, including each of us, in the same way. There is, in the end, one force, one spirit, that works in all of the universe. The chemicals in our hands and those in our brains were forged in the same furnace that forged the stars. The same spirit that drives oxygen to unite with hydrogen makes a baby cry when it is hungry, sends the adolescent out in hormonal restlessness, and calls Mother Teresa to a church to pray. (*The Holy Longing*, 18)

It appears that the spiritual journey is seeing how God is calling us to greater integration with others, the world, and God's own self through that energy. Amazing!

Even more awesome for us is the reality that our unobservable fleck of life hanging onto a far-flung planet is personally known and loved by God. That's *you*! In fact, every breath, every heartbeat (100,000 per day), every movement that we make is utterly, totally dependent on God's continual extension of his existence to us, and so too is everything else in the entire universe. All of life is cradled in and infused with God's presence, God's power, God's love. Even more startling, God is intimately forming and calling us to join with him in the divine work of creating, living, loving.

Examen S.T.R.I.P.

I wonder if Jacques Marquette looked up at this same sky on the first night of his journey and contemplated his place in the world given the vastness of the starry heavens. If he did, my guess is that he ruminated about how human beings are totally insignificant in the vastness of the created world, and yet fully loved by God, who intentionally created each one of us. Such reflection would not be surprising for a Jesuit immersed within Ignatian spirituality, particularly since the *Spiritual Exercises* are premised on the assumption that the only way we can come into an authentic, full relationship with God is to recognize our proper nature and place in the created order. As is true with any bond of love, a *genuine* relationship with God is not possible unless it is built on the true knowledge of one's identity or place in life and acceptance of the reality of God's marvelous gift.

While such reflection on the part of Marquette would be in harmony with his spiritual outlook, in the end we simply do not know what Marquette thought about that night on the river. All his journal tells us about that first day is this:

> The river on which we embarked is called Meskousing [the Wisconsin]. It is very wide and has a sandy bottom that forms various shoals that make navigation very difficult. It is full of islands covered with vines. On the banks one sees fertile land, with woods, prairies, and hills succeeding one another. There is oak, walnut, and basswood trees; and another kind, whose branches are armed with long thorns. We saw there neither feathered game nor fish, but many deer and a large number of cattle [bison]. (*JR*, 194)

But we can be sure about two things. First, this intrepid band slept on one of these islands, just as we are doing. Marquette records later in his journal that they never slept on the shore, but always slept in the middle of the river out of fear of the Lakota. The second surety regarding that first night is that Marquette prayed the evening Examen ("examination") of Consciousness. Saint Ignatius insisted that the Examen should never be skipped by a Jesuit, no matter how busy he might be during the day or how tired he might be at night.

Why is the Examen so important in Ignatian spirituality? Because its practice properly places us in our lives, at that very moment, and then it properly points us to where God is leading us. In the creative process called life, God is perpetually inviting us into relationship. However, this relationship can only be full, authentic, and complete to the degree that we live our life in a manner consistent with the way we are made. As previously discussed, our desires are meant to lead us to God, but they also can blind us to the way of God. We humans tend to hunt for love in the wrong ways and places. This desire for love can lead us to seek completeness by puffing up our pride, wholeness by striving for control, or happiness by chasing sensual pleasures. Ignatius' Examen offers a very practical and potent method of prayer that helps us reflect on and properly order our desires so that every day we might better orient our lives in relation to that First Principle and Foundation.

What is the Examen? You might say it is about doing "inscape" work by taking a look at the landscape of our daily lives. The Examen encourages us to retaste and refeel the day in the presence of God by reflecting on all the things that made us laugh, cry, sad, angry, joyful, and so forth. Notice, this is *not* an examination of conscience, which is a way of recounting sins in preparation for the sacrament of reconciliation. Instead, in the Examen we allow the activity of God in our lives to become apparent and to expose us to a marvelous fact: no matter where we have been in our day's journey, God was there, directly speaking to us through our experience.

The point of the Examen, therefore, is to allow the movement of God to soften our hearts. The Examen, says J. J. O'Leary, teaches us that "[o]ur hearts are like putty—if you knead putty it stays soft; if you don't, it becomes hard and impossible to move. By quietly going over the events of a day, we keep our heart soft, our minds aware, and our vision open to the presence of others—and of the Lord" ("A Short Course on Prayer," 11–12). By prayerfully "massaging" the events of a day, the Spirit keeps our hearts pliable so that they might become ever-more conformed to the form of divine love.

Several different translations and versions of the Examen exist, but the following is a very simple, "stripped-down" version (it even uses the acronym S.T.R.I.P. in the title). Not only does this acronym serve as a mnemonic for the various steps in this prayer process, but it also has the double meaning: (1) it encourages us to "strip" down all of our motivations, interactions, and inclinations so that (2) we can see our lives in the naked (authentic, bare, or "stripped") light of God's love. In other words, we must remove the masks that cover our joys and fears and thus allow God's grace to transform us more fully into the person whom God has made (and continues to make) us to be. So you might say the Examen is both bluff and buff!

Of course, this self-exposure is the purpose of all prayer, not just the Examen. Prayer is about vulnerably and authenticity, about placing ourselves before God by stripping away our self-centered demands. In our marriage preparation work, my wife and I have been struck by the fact that engaged couples invariably have a much easier time talking about their sexual experiences than they do about their prayer lives. At first I was disheartened by this observation, but then I realized that their reaction reveals a profound truth: authentic prayer is more intimate than sex because we expose our naked souls.

By walking through this prayer method for about ten minutes a day, we can allow God to direct and orient us on the life's daily journey through our desires.

Examen S.T.R.I.P.

1. _S_ettle: Quieting your spirit, take a few minutes to become aware of God's presence.
2. _T_hank: After briefly bringing them to mind, thank God for the gifts and graces of this day.
3. _R_ecall: Ruminate over the events of your day—your social interactions, inner thoughts, emotional responses, particular behaviors. Re-experience your day in your imagination, freely allowing the feelings of these events to bubble up to

your consciousness. Be aware of any movements of consolation or desolation as you review your day. Where was God in all this—what was "of God" and what was "not of God"? Put another way: where did you love well, and where did you stifle love in yourself or in others?

4. Interact: Talk with God about the grist of this review of your day. Focus upon the event or pattern—whether one of consolation or desolation—that tugs most strongly upon your heart or conscience. Thank God for any insights and, if necessary, ask God's forgiveness for any sins of commission or omission.

5. Plan: Make specific resolutions for the future: how you will handle a particular situation better in the future, how you will find God in the events on tomorrow's daily calendar and the persons you will encounter during the course of the next day.

As you do the Examen, remember one thing: prayer is not something you do, as much as something you are in. It is, as some have called it, *the life in the gaze:* the gaze of God. So do not mistake the Examen as being about resolutions. It is ultimately a position; a vantage point; a way of seeing the self, others, and God in perspective. It is less about words spoken and more about placement—becoming aware that one's life is held in God's warmhearted look so that our wills might meld within divine love. In a nutshell, the Examen is a habit of attention brought to bear on all that is. As a prayer method, it is a means of channeling that divine creative energy so that we might, quite simply, place ourselves on the Great River.

Snake Encounter

David and I awaken in the morning with a start when our make-shift tent collapses on us. As we struggle to free ourselves, we pick up the laughter of the previous night. We are impressed that our shelter waited until 7:00 AM before quitting.

A beautiful mist hangs on the river. The only sounds are those of excited morning birds and the hum of industrious flying insects. A glorious morning!

We eat breakfast, pack the canoe, and shove off. Our plans have changed somewhat due to the tent situation. We had originally planned to paddle leisurely downriver until we found a good camping spot, which we expected would be just a couple miles short of the Spring Green landing, our takeout destination. But now we will paddle a bit more aggressively all the way to the landing, so that I can take our car (which the shuttle service transported to this spot) into town and buy a tent.

It is another wonderful day. Bright and sunny. Too cool for a swim, but perfect for paddling. The wind is still at our backs, so we make good time. But we also take the time to enjoy the noble beauty of the landscape, the lavish blue of the sky, and the tranquil spirit of the river.

As noon approaches, we pick out an inviting island for lunch. We tie the canoe to a washed-up tree now consisting of only a hollow trunk. We carry our lunch supplies to the shore and enjoy a relaxing, simple meal.

After brief naps on the warm sand in the embracing sun, we reload the canoe. David, carrying our folding camp chairs, decides to access the canoe by walking through the water side of the long-dead tree trunk. Suddenly, I hear the tide of quick-stirred water. I turn to see David—backpedaling away from the trunk, his burdened arms flailing as he tries to keep his balance. The river's resistant current and uneven sand bottom win this battle as he plops down. I start to chuckle. But then he scrambles up, moving quickly toward shore.

"There's a snake! There's a snake on that log," he sputters. Always the courageous one, I ask, "Is it still there?" as I take a couple steps backward. The inevitable answer comes back, "I don't know."

We move stealthily toward the tree trunk. An 18-inch loop of a snake's thick body is protruding from a crack in the hollowed-out tree, but the head and tail are inside the trunk. The body consists of red, black, brown, and white bands. I frantically search my "snake-identification memory bank" for information about the color coding of poisonous snakes, and then realize that I can't tell a garter snake from a water moccasin. I do know one thing: there are no water moccasins in Wisconsin. But there are rattlesnakes.

Then David says, "It looks kind of dead." It does indeed have a sort of gray, limp look to it. "You think it is?" I ask. We inch closer, trying to discern its status as a living being. We cast some pebbles at the tree. The snake's body does not move. We inch closer, shouting "Hey, snake!" (as if it knew its name) to see if it moves. Nothing. Again, always the courageous one, I say to Dave, "Hit the log with that folding chair." Dave looks at me incredulously, and we have the inevitable "You do it; no, you do it" banter.

Finally, David creeps forward, stretches out, and lightly knocks the log with the folding chair. Again, nothing. Now fully emboldened, David strides up to the tree and confidently hits the tree with a solid stroke. The snake suddenly slithers inside the hollow log. Now we are both doing the frantic "backpedal stroke"! We laugh at our faint-heartedness.

After we collect ourselves, we realize that stirring the snake had created a dilemma. Is the snake still in the log, or did it exit? If it left the log, did it go out the side near our canoe and is now moving freely through the water? Skirting the log as much as possible, we continually scan the ground and water as we finish loading the canoe. We quickly hop in and cast off from shore, happy to be safely back on the river.

Soaring Eagles

We continue downriver without incident. Once we arrive at the Spring Green landing, I buzz into town and buy a new dome tent at the sporting goods store and then return to the river. We shove back into the river and paddle downstream about a half mile to a nice island. We camp on the west side so that the island's trees won't inhibit our view of the sunset. As we set up the new tent, it does not take much to get us giggling again as we recall our golf net affair.

Given the previous night's shelter issues, it is somewhat ironic that we are camped this night about a mile from Taliesin, the family home of the famous architect, Frank Lloyd Wright. Wright's innovative design philosophy sprang from the important lessons he learned on the banks of the Wisconsin River. He believed that people are most content and happy when they live in harmony with nature rather than imposing their will upon it. Inventing the "organic architecture" style, he became the most influential architect of the twentieth century, as evidenced by the fact that more than one-third of all the buildings he designed are listed on the National Register of Historic Places.

As an adult, Wright built a house on Taliesin and founded his influential architecture school on its grounds so that his students also could learn from the river. He wanted them to learn to see that a house should not be *on* a hill, plain, or river, but *of* it—belonging to it. The only way that lesson can be learned is by becoming so surrounded by nature that you come to understand your place in creation. As he was fond of saying, "No stream rises higher than its source. What ever man might build could never express or reflect more than he was. He could record neither more nor less than he had learned of life when the buildings were built"(www .cmgww.com/historic/flw/quotes.html). Certainly, this is true not only of building buildings but also of living one's own life.

Once we organize our camp and eat dinner, we do some fishing. We have some good luck. Our foresight in choosing this place is rewarded: the sunset is spectacular! Streaking purples, splashing oranges, dashing yellows. I stop fishing to look at my son, fishing on the western-most point of the island, framed within that horizon of grace. It is good.

The moment is interrupted by the shrill ringing of David's cell phone. He answers it, reeling in his line as he talks. He sets his pole against a log and walks up the beach, searching for better reception. The call is from a friend in New York City who has been commissioned to find an apartment for David. Suddenly, his impending departure from home, just a few weeks away, breaks the magical feel of that night.

After an extended conversation, David hangs up and excitedly reports, "Well, I've got my new place all set up. It's located across the river from Manhattan in Hoboken, New Jersey. It's just an efficiency apartment, but it'll do. What's way cool about this place is that it's just a block away from the subway stop. The subway goes under the river and comes out on the Manhattan side, a block from my place of work. Is that great or what!"

What do I say to my son? On the practical, convenience side of things, it is "way cool." But from the metaphorical, spiritual perspective, I want to shout: "Never, never try to make it through life by going under the river, or over it, or even through it. No, there's only one way to travel the river...*with* it. For then you are framed in the glorious light of God. *That* is your place...*on* the river." And that *is* complete and great!

But instead, I hold my tongue—both because I know that is not what he is talking about and because I know that my job now is to support and encourage him. Ultimately, he will have to make the lessons of the river his own. He will have to struggle with the river in his own time before he comes to understand his place in it. Just as Marquette did so long ago, it is now time for him to step boldly into the unknown, for only then can he discover whether and how the river flows to the Immense Water...to God.

Living within the canyons of man-made skyscrapers, though, can quickly disorient one's sense of bearing, one's understanding of one's place in this world. So I hope that this trip through God's wondrous creation somehow "inoculates" him. No, that's not the right word. Rather, I hope it *connects* him to...well, to the *really* real. That it's a glimpse of seeing...the reality of all. Even now I can't describe it, capture it, or communicate it. It's like water...so real, yet impossible to hold in the hand because it slips through the fingers of tangible expression.

So I must borrow another's words—the words of Aldo Leopold, the great naturalist who lived in this part of Wisconsin and the author of the classic, *A Sand County Almanac*.

> Possibly, in our intuitive perceptions, which may be truer than our science and less impeded by words than our philosophies, we realize the indivisibility of the earth— its soil, mountains, rivers, forest, climate, plants, and animals, and respect it collectively not only as a useful servant but as a living being, vastly less alive than ourselves in degree, but vastly greater than ourselves in time and space—a being that was old when the morning stars sang together and, when the last of us has been gathered unto his fathers, will still be young. (Leopold, quoted in Metcoff, *Along the Wisconsin Riverway*)

But even Leopold's words are insufficient. There is more to it. It's not just about experiencing the oneness of nature. It is also about knowing, seeing, and perceiving that one is enfolded within the hands of God.

The next morning, we break camp and paddle back upstream to the Spring Green landing. We are ending this first leg of the journey—June 1—on the same day that Jacques Marquette's life began three hundred sixty-eight years ago. I goad David into singing a hearty version of "Happy Birthday, Jacques" as we paddle. Just then, two bald eagles appear and circle endlessly on the warm air currents. The Native Americans consider the appearance of bald eagles a positive omen, for it shows the presence of a good and powerful spirit.

> *And though the last lights off the black West went*
>   *Oh, morning, at the brown brink eastward,*
>   *springs—*
> *Because the Holy Ghost over the bent*
>   *World broods with warm breast and with ah!*
> *Bright wings.* (Hopkins, "God's Grandeur")

Hopkins is right. I smile. I started this trip fearing that I have given my son a paddle that was too short for his new journey ahead. But I end this leg of the Russell River Rendezvous with a calm reassurance in the Spirit's bright wings. Surely God is in this place and in all places.

So now it is almost time for me to say goodbye to my son as he starts his own adventure. And I will say that word with full gusto. For *goodbye* is actually a contraction for "God be with you." Over the years, the "be with you" part of the phrase was verbally shortened to "be 'ye" and finally "bye"—and "God" became "good." The French word *adieu* and the Spanish *adiós* have similar religious connotations of placing the person into God's care, although they literally mean "to God." So, raw as it might be, *goodbye* will be exactly the *correct* word to say to my son in a few short weeks. After all, the first God Question is all about discovering this simple point: God is with us.

Goodbye, son.

CHAPTER TWO

Who Is God Calling Us to Be?

What is our place in the world?
Who is God calling us to be?
How is God caring for us?
Where is God's love?

Calling Scout

"Come here, Scout! Get in the canoe. Let's go. Scout! Come *here!*" My pleadings raise her head from the river's edge, but then the puppy dashes farther down the bank. My youngest son Ian and I give chase. Mid-July might be the dog days of summer, but this is ridiculous.

The great Russell River Rendezvous is about to embark on its second leg...*if* we can corral this barking dog and get her into the canoe. Scout, a German shepherd–hound mix, is the newest addition to the household. Two weeks earlier at the Humane Society, the boys cajoled my wife and me into adopting this lanky five-month-old canine with such a sorrowful face.

We planned to get a dog that summer because our previous one, an ancient warrior older than our youngest child, died some months earlier. David's move to New York City pushed us to act quicker and more impulsively than planned. After David left, the house seemed oddly quiet and more empty than usual. I say "odd" because in a sense nothing really changed. David had already been out of the house during the past four school years, so his absence wasn't really new. Yet, it was different now: more quiet and empty.

What better way to fill that space than with a bounding, rambunctious puppy! Ian particularly bonded with Scout, who was named after the little girl in the classic, *To Kill a Mockingbird*. The dog's name had been hotly debated. Everyone wanted a name descriptive of her personality, yet the boys were hesitant to focus too much on her "feminine" side. The "Scout" moniker won because it was sufficiently masculine for the sons and literarily substantial enough for the parents.

Ian and I finally lure Scout to the canoe using a bit of reverse psychology. We start running *away* from her, toward the canoe. Sensing a game, Scout gives chase. As she comes near, I grab her by the collar, but she resists getting into the rocking boat. So I lift her up and place her on the packs in the middle. This will be her "throne" for the journey; all the canoe's floor space is occupied by camping equipment or our legs.

Before Scout can abandon ship, we quickly shove off from the Spring Green landing, the same spot where David and I had ended our leg of the journey. Now Ian and I begin our part of this adventure of reduplicating the Marquette-Jolliet journey down the River of Discovery to the Mississippi.

Naming River

I'm trying to avoid calling the river "the Wisconsin" because I've uncovered a disappointing fact. Captivated by the river after the first leg of the journey, I started reading about its history during the six weeks since my trip with David. Evidently it is now disputed that "Wisconsin" derives from a Native American word that means "The Gathering of Waters." The heart of the debate revolves around Marquette's French phonetic spelling of the river's name "Meskousing," which was later reproduced in the first published account of the Marquette-Jolliet expedition as "Mescousin" and eventually morphed among the American settlers into "Wisconsin." The linguistic analysis is convoluted—and complicated since we do not know if Marquette was replicating an Algonquian or Miami term for this river—but now the dominant scholarly opinion seems to be that the word means "River by the Red Rock" or "river running through a red place."

When I read that, I felt like Charlie Brown trick-or-treating on Halloween night. There is a certain romance and drama to a river named "The Gathering of Waters." It has a mystic ring to it, and it is the perfect metaphor for this trip with my sons. But "River by the Red Rock"? What a letdown. Let's face it: the rock image only takes you so far. After all, this is a journey about water—about staying with the fluid questions on the moving river. And now I learn that the river's very name is about the *shore*—about the deceptive answers of inflexible stone. I want water, but I got a rock.

Well, as Marquette would have said in French, *"C'est la vie"* ("that's life"). On one level, it's inconsequential. Yet, as we begin our journey, I can't shrug it off. Names *do* matter. The power of a name is not to be underestimated. Psychologists tell us that names directly affect personality development because they influence people's perceptions and reactions to the individual. As parents, we take the right of naming our children quite seriously. We buy books that list and explain the meanings of names, cull through family history to uncover various traditional names, and finally test numerous options before each child's birth. How we are named goes to the heart of the second God Question: *Who is God calling us to be?* How we engage that question affects the nature of our river journey.

A few years earlier, Ian had become quite captivated with the process by which he was named. He had peppered my wife and me with numerous questions: Why did we name him *Ian*?

Who first came up with the idea of calling him by that name? What would we have called him if he had been a girl? Why did we give the names we did to his older brothers? The questions rolled on and on. At about the same age, in that transition period from grade school to junior high, my other three sons also wanted to discover the reasons for their names. I suppose this is because children enter a new level of consciousness about their self-identity at that crucial age. Times of transition are periods of renegotiated character.

As I look at Ian's straining back as he paddles, I wonder if I have ever given my youngest son a complete answer to his many questions. If I think about it, I don't simply call him "Ian." I have other names for him. I have some funny nicknames like "E-Man" and simply "E," which he has heard numerous times. But there are many tender terms for him within my heart that I have never spoken to him: "My Fearless Kind-Hearted One" and "Energizing-Presence-With-Sparkling-Eyes." These names do not simply label him but reveal what I reverence in him.

I should tell Ian—and all my sons—these other deeply felt names that I have for them. I should share them because they have a power to them. The names by which we designate each other have power because they elicit responses from within us. Calling you by name means you are called for something. Names change us.

Missioning Name

Scripture tells us that God knows about the power of names in the presence of rivers. The gospels portray Jesus' baptism at the Jordan River as a sort of "naming ceremony." At first blush that last statement seems to topple from the rhetorical to the ridiculous. Naming ceremony? What are you talking about? Jesus already had a name before his baptism: Jesus, his name was Jesus! However, in Mark, Matthew, and Luke, the gospels that narrate Jesus' baptism, the voice from the heavens proclaims: "You are my beloved Son, with you I am well pleased" (Luke 3:22, *NAB*). At that moment, we learn that the Father has another name for Jesus: Beloved-Son-Who-Fulfills.

I'm sure Jesus' sense of self was changed—transformed—when he heard God the Father call him "beloved Son" at his baptism. This naming incident was so consequential that Jesus immediately departs on a journey into the desert. Mark's Gospel even insinuates that Jesus flees in some consternation, for it describes the Spirit as driving him forward. In this place of red rock and dry dust, Jesus encounters the temptation to abandon the water by rejecting the challenging questions embedded within the Father's fond expression for him. In the end, Jesus chooses instead to embrace his name by living within its misty implications. Notice that the name does not signify a new relationship or quality of being; Jesus had always been the Son of God; Christ is the Second Person of the Trinity. Rather, the pronouncement of that name itself leads Jesus to his core mission. That woolly name christens him to be who he was in a new way. Thus, Mark and Matthew report that Jesus leaves the barren wilderness and returns to bracing water, for he goes directly to the Sea of Galilee, the source of the Jordan River, to begin his vocation of ushering in the Kingdom of God by calling forth—by name—his apostles.

Likewise, the second God Question calls us forth to live as disciples in a manner that joins us with this in-breaking of the kingdom of God. At our own baptisms, our parents—in response to the priest's question, "What name have you chosen for this child?"—informed the community how we are to be known. However, our faith tells us that by our baptisms we are also God's children. So this means that God must also have special, loving names for us because he knows the very soul—the essence—of who we are.

Here is the kicker: how God names us also calls us to our mission in life because the speaking of a name implicitly calls for a response by the person named. This double-edged significance of name-calling is captured in the word *vocation,* derived from a Latin word *(vocāre)* that means "to call," but which signifies in English the work or passion of our lives. So the call of God never ends with the simple uttering of our name. Rather, we are always called to something. God's name for us calls us to be sent…to be *apostles,* which literally means "one who is sent."

So we should not flippantly or lightly ask the second God Question because the answer requires something of us; this question even chased Jesus off the river and into the desert! But if we are bold enough to wade into the scary depth of the second God Question, then ponder this: What are the names by which God knows you—and what do they call out of you? Could they be: "My Compassionate One, go and heal those who are suffering," or "My Beloved, go and care for the children," or "My Inquisitive One, go and discover," or "My Champion of Justice, go and proclaim the truth." This "Go and _____" is our vocation. Our vocations are simply our response to the call of our Lover, God. It is not a job or a role. It is a calling of God.

However, we are not just called as individuals but in community. The word for "church" in Greek, the language of the New Testament, literally translated means "the called." What is the name by which God calls us as a community? We commonly refer to ourselves as Christians, but the early followers of Christ did not use that name; that was the name the Romans used for them. Rather, the Acts of the Apostles and the Didache (a very early Christian writing) name them as "People of the Way." This is our true family name.

Because we don't use our original Christian surname anymore, we often contort our name into the "People of Heavenly Destiny." But destiny is about predetermination, not indetermination. It is about answers, not questions. It is no surprise that the words *destiny* and *destination* are linguistically related; they describe the cessation of a journey, not the journey itself. But our last name, the People of the Way, distinguishes us as those who view faith as an ongoing process.

The metaphor of *journey* quickly became a definitional image for Christians. All four gospel writers use travel narratives to structure their stories about Jesus. Some may say that this is because Jesus did wander Palestine as he taught and healed. This is undoubtedly historically true, but some noncanonical gospels (early accounts of Jesus that were not included in the Bible) never mention Jesus' travels. Instead, they recount his words and miracles as if he stayed in one spot. Thus one need not automatically assume that the only way to teach about Jesus is by recounting his journeys throughout Palestine. For example, Paul never mentions Jesus' travels (although he mentions his own) in his letters to the first Christian communities. However, the very fact that the only gospels accepted into the Bible were those that focused heavily on Jesus' various travels indicates that *journey* was a constitutive element in envisioning the faithful way of being and existing for early Christians.

What are we called to be and do if we have indeed been named the People of the Way? First, it means that we are a pilgrim people—a group on a journey, not folks who have already arrived at a destination. Second, we must understand that *discipleship* is a verb, not a noun. It is not about concrete convictions or reified rubrics, but about animated action. So an authentic engagement with the second God Question properly identifies the nature of Christian faith, as well as our individual vocations. In both cases, our names don't give us a destiny but send us on a mission. We are sent. We are apostles. What's in a name? Only God's loving will for us.

Reading Signs

Scout is not adjusting well to canoe travel. She is discombobulated by the canoe's rocking, caused by her pacing on the packs. She whines and looks anxious. Ian turns and tries to soothe her. "It's OK, girl. Settle down, Scout." His efforts eventually succeed. Scout curls up on top of the packs and starts to enjoy the view. Worn out by her earlier frantic efforts, she even begins to nap.

The weather is not stellar. It is overcast with a slight drizzle. The sun only peaks out periodically from the gray clouds. But the unusually cool July weather certainly makes paddling easier. In contrast to the mediocre weather, the scenery is spectacular. This section of the river is quite striking with its towering bluffs and attractive islands. Ian and I are in good spirits.

As we go farther downstream, Ian yells back to me, "Hey, Dad. Look up there. There are some cows in the river!" Sure enough, about half a dozen Holsteins are wallowing in the stream, having evidently found a break in the barbed-wire fence that runs parallel to the river about twenty-five yards back in the woods. We drift by the disinterested cows, grateful that Scout is sleeping.

As we pass, I use the event as an entrée for discussing Marquette's journey with Ian. "Marquette saw his first buffalo along this river," I offer, "although he called them 'cattle' in his journal. He was the first European to write a first-hand description of the buffalo and the herds, one of which he numbered at four hundred head." As the band of explorers moved deeper into the unknown, strange land, Marquette's attempt to mediate his experience of the river journey through the language of his past becomes evident in his description of the buffalo, analyzing every feature in comparison to "cattle," "oxen," "horses," and even "sheep" (*JR*, 195).

I guess that is what we all try to do, even today: understand where we are through the lenses of where we have been. Maybe Marquette's way of deciphering the present in light of the past is not surprising given that his spiritual mentor, Ignatius, instilled this same approach to one's spiritual life. As David Fleming so aptly notes:

> Ignatius carefully directs our attention to looking back so that we might look forward. It is by reflecting on our past experience and seeing how God has been active, or perhaps how we have ignored God, that we are sensitized to seeing the divinely patterned paths which lead over the horizon of our vision. For Ignatius, there is only one place for us to start in our discernment process: We must reflect on our past experience and trace the patterns of God in our life. In fact, for Ignatius the daily examen was a continual check on our "discerning" way of living. (*Like the Lightning*, 136)

Stated another way, we see God's movement in our lives primarily by looking in the rearview mirror. In fact, looking backward is often how we hear God within the second God Question. Through an intentional engagement with our past by praying with the Examen, we hear God whispering our name within the discerned patterns of our lives. And the name sends us forward in mission.

Past experience helps me better navigate the river on this leg of the journey. The Wisconsin's main channel is relatively deep, but it is also a broad river. Thus, if you wander outside the main channel, it is easy enough to paddle into shallow shoals. Then the canoe becomes grounded and there is no recourse but to get out of the boat and walk it back to deeper water. In his journal, Marquette noted that this feature of the river made it hard to navigate, and I am sure that now and again he and his six companions had to hop out of their two birch-bark canoes to return to the deep running waters.

Since Ian is in front, his eyes are crucial if we are to avoid this fate. So I give him a clue for locating the deep water. "Look for dark water because that is a sign that it's deeper there." However, this piece of advice evidently is not sufficient as we soon run aground. Ian is baffled, "What happened? I could see that the water was running really fast here. It was all ripply, like rapids." So I offer another rule for deciphering the ways of the river: "The sand bottom is so near the surface that it makes the water ripple like that. Remember the old saying, 'Still water runs deep.'" Ian looks back at me, puzzled. "What does that mean?" "Well," I answer, "It means that the deeper water looks like it isn't moving, although the current is actually stronger there." Ian is skeptical. "That can't be right. If the water is moving fast, you should be able to see the water moving." I smile and simply say, "You'll see what I mean after a while." Still fighting the counterintuitive nature of my advice, Ian periodically directs us into shallow water.

Clearly my wise advice is not effective in instructing my son on the ways of the river. Then I devise a better approach: observational experience. I say to him, "I tell you what, Ian. Let's not paddle for awhile. We'll just let the river push us along." This suggestion is warmly welcomed because Ian is happy to take a break. We sweep along in gentle "S's," carried in the roving but strong main current. Only after a while do I return to active coaching. I do not give Ian more hard rules, but some flowing questions: "As we drift along here, Ian, watch the water that is all around us. What color is it? What is its texture—smooth or ripply? Do we ever get beached if we stay in this dark, placid-looking water? Just watch the river for the answers." After a while, we start paddling again. Now Ian follows the path of the still, dark, strong water. There are a few more miscues; his untrained eyes are still learning to discern the more subtle movements of the water. But the truth of the water is now known. Ian becomes a good navigator and a believer in deep, still waters.

Hiding Stone

About seven miles into our journey, we approach the town of Lone Rock, set back about a half-mile from the river. The town was named for an unusual stone formation (again with the rocks!) on the north bank. The formation was an important landmark for the early river hogs who navigated these waters. Although it was helpful in plotting a course on the river, the town folk prized its sandstone as a building material. Over the years, they whittled it down to build the Congregational church and surrounding houses until its presence on the river's horizon was completely erased.

Now the truth of that story is "rock solid," but there are many other legendary yarns about this stretch of the river, especially concerning buried treasure in the bluffs. There is the tale of the steamboat, bound for Fort Winnebago near Portage, that became hopelessly beached near Lone Rock. The crew abandoned ship, but they supposedly buried the chest of gold coins containing the soldiers' pay before they attempted to walk through the hostile Indian territory. As the story goes, the sailors never returned to civilization, but a map indicating the buried chest's location survived. As you might guess, this treasure map has been periodically "found"...and sold to eager but naïve fortune hunters.

Then there are the stories of Bogus Bluff, located about another seven miles downriver from Lone Rock. In the 1850s local newspapers were full of stories about a supposedly immense cache of gold that the Indians stockpiled in a secret cave. One of Bogus Bluff's many caves also purportedly serves as the depository for a Chicago gang's hidden stash of counterfeit bills, still unclaimed because the mob was arrested and imprisoned before they could retrieve their ill-produced property. Even Bogus Bluff's name comes from a story of lost wealth: the early settlers thought they had struck it rich when they mistook its yellow rock for gold. These are just a few of the tantalizing stories about misplaced treasures in these bluffs.

As we approach Lone Rock, we come upon a large island, accurately but blandly named Long Island, that obscures the view down the river. Our guidebook advises us to hug the south side of the island, as it is easy at this point to assume that the main channel is farther to the left—but that leads you into a marshy bay leading up Otter Creek. If only life came with a handbook or map so we could avoid wrong turns, shallow fantasies, and bad choices.

Guiding Water

Fortunately, God equipped us with an innate awareness by which we can indeed discern the fitting course, but we rarely recognize its presence because we get bluffed into hunting for answers in life's dark crevices, not in the life-giving water. The question of the river, the second God Question, is *"Who is God calling us to be?"* Unfortunately, we often mistakenly phrase it as a "rock" question: What does God want me to do with my life? On one level, that is not necessarily a bad question, as it can, to a degree, help us negotiate life. But it focuses on *doing* rather than *being*. Thus, we tend to construct our lives with the answer, not live our lives in the midst of the question. So the guiding question disappears as we carve it into the shape of firm, rocklike certainty (the answer).

Any talk of "God's plan for me" is bound to run us ashore because it gives the impression that God holds some sort of treasure map as the key to my happiness—and that the "goal" of life is simply to find where God has hidden my particular treasure map. Well, God is not a sadistic pirate! God is really quite transparent about the whole happiness thing because the Bible is rather clear: "God is love, and those who abide in love abide in God, and God abides in them" (1 John 4:16). That's God's will for you, and God probably has devised thousands of plans on how to live in that love. There is *one* will, but *thousands* of plans!

Marquette traveled these same waters knowing this fundamental truth; it is the heart of Ignatian spirituality. Saint Ignatius learned it by looking in the rearview mirror of his own life journey. His powerful conversion experience led him to believe that God was calling him to live in the Holy Land. Unfortunately, he was not granted permission by the Pope, so he was redirected home by the Franciscans. He felt God direct him to study in the universities at Alcalá and Salamanca. But then the Inquisition forced him out of these towns. He gathered a small band of like-minded, dedicated men who also felt moved by the Spirit to return to the Holy Land, but again their passage was denied. Believing that God is in all things, Ignatius still saw the presence of God in all of his travels. After every thwarted step, he was convinced he was fulfilling God's will. As one path closed, Ignatius chose another, fully confident that he was following one of God's thousands of plans for him because he was living in God's love.

Think of it this way. Let's say you want to go by river from the state of Wisconsin to the Atlantic Ocean. Every river in Wisconsin ultimately gets to the Atlantic Ocean. As Marquette discovered, some flow into the Wisconsin River, then into the Mississippi, and end in the Atlantic Ocean's Gulf of Mexico. Other rivers run toward Lake Michigan, which joins the Atlantic by way of the other Great Lakes and the St. Lawrence Seaway. Even if you go against the current of the river, as Marquette did until he reached the Wisconsin River, and portage from one river to the next, ultimately all the rivers flow into the ocean.

So which is the "right" river? They are all the right river if your one goal is to reach the Atlantic Ocean because they all will get you there. Why should you prefer a long river over a short one; they are all ways to your destination! There is only one rule: you must, sooner or later, let go of yourself to allow the current of God's love to pull and bear you. Only in this manner can we start to discern the color and texture of the current of God's love in the world.

Consoling Spirit

The key to recognizing the pattern in the water of life is tapping into what Ignatius called the experiences of consolation and desolation. Ignatius realized this as he was laid up in a castle, recovering from a cannonball injury incurred during a battle with the French. Until he suffered this war wound, Ignatius had been something of a rogue as a young man and his main goal was to seek glory and wealth.

Ignatius' recovery was slow and tedious, and at one point he almost died. Seeking to divert his attention, Ignatius asked for books with stories of romance and chivalry. You know the stuff: stories of damsels in distress and wearing low-cut dresses; tales of knights in tights and in high-risk adventures. But the only books in the castle were on the lives of the saints and the life of Christ.

At first Ignatius scoffed at such religious tomes but ultimately his boredom eroded his resistance and he started to read these "paltry" offerings. Startlingly, Ignatius found himself daydreaming about imitating the exploits of the saints in their devotion to following Jesus, although he also still fantasized about winning fame and wooing women as a knight. However, he was struck by the difference in the emotional effect of these flights of imagination. After reading and reflecting on the lives of the saints and Christ, Ignatius felt content, exhilarated, and energized—and this feeling stayed with him long after he had finished reading. In contrast, while he was "charged up" when actively daydreaming about pursuing his former life at court, afterward he found himself restless, discontented, and despondent. Ignatius called the former experience *consolation* and the latter *desolation*. He realized that God speaks directly through these affective reactions. God was drawing him through his authentic desires.

Notice that Ignatius sees God as revealing himself because this feeling of consolation lasts longer—it lingers and infuses him—than desolation. So the distinction between consolation and desolation is not necessarily that one feels "good" and the other "bad." Rather, it is more about the effect on the affect. Consolation provides illumination, a palpable sense of God's presence, an impulse to do good deeds, a joy in self-sacrificing, a confidence in knowing that you are in the right place doing the right thing even in the midst of hardship. Desolation feels like you are just going through the motions, attracted to the distasteful instead of the fulfilling, apathetic toward success or failure, or just living in a spiritual gray zone. In both cases, consolation and desolation work on the feelings more through the heart than the head. Ignatius identifies the dynamic between consolation and desolation as the "discernment of spirits."

Not surprisingly, discernment of spirits lies at the foundation of Ignatius' personal conversion and the entire *Spiritual Exercises.* According to Ignatius, God leads us through these affective movements of the Spirit into the direction of love. Love can only exist in a relationship, not in the abstract, so we move from a human (often selfish) way of looking at things into a way of understanding our place in the world through our love of God in Christ. This relationship of love is so intense that we take on the mind and heart of Christ. When this is achieved, says Ignatius, our life becomes more about *coming into* a choice than about making decisions. Thus, the discernment of spirits is fundamentally about relationship, not choice or decision.

While Ignatius' prayerful discernment of spirits led him to abandon his former life and undertake a new path of radical discipleship, he proclaimed that God works with each of us directly and individually in accordance with how God made us, that is, through our uniquely authentic desires. Hence, someone else in Ignatius' situation might feel a sense of consolation after fantasizing about the life of a knight and desolation when contemplating the radical lifestyle of the saints. This may be a sign that God was calling that person to a secular, nonreligious profession as the means by which to serve and love God. Everyone is called differently. We are not all called, like Ignatius, to abandon everything and adopt a new "religious" way of life.

Each of our vocations may differ, but we are all the same in this truth: God keeps filling us with gifts and desires. We are continually called to love God, to be in relationship, which helps us to make choices, decisions, and to take action. For some of us, our relationship with God might lead us to a radical shift in life priorities; for most, however, it involves more subtle changes in our behaviors and attitudes so that we more firmly and faithfully live our present vocation as friend, spouse, parent, employee, student, reformer, leader, and so forth.

Since we are talking about loving more fully, our call does involve cultivating an active Ignatian "indifference"; Christ's love moves within desire (*eros*) into self-sacrifice (*agape*). It involves letting go—letting the river's current carry us. Joseph Tetlow captured this movement quite exquisitely:

> Conscious of the high adventure, sublime destiny, and eternal freedom for which each of us was created—and of the vocation to which God invites each of us—we seek a deep-felt sense of surrender. Only in our cooperative surrender does God have the freedom to mold us in His likeness. We are partners, God and we, in the continual process of our becoming. Thus, every day there is a decision, a will, a choice to be made. We may feel a need for change in the ways we have chosen in the past. We turn to God for direction by surrendering to God's will. (Tetlow, *Choosing Christ in the World*)

Ignatius understood that God's will is ultimately to love us and to foster love. Hence, obedience to God's will is not blind submission, but rather active *listening* and responding to God's love for us. Thus, doing the will of God is more about loving better than with doing the right thing.

Unlike we modern American individualists, though, Ignatius

was much more comfortable with conceiving God as speaking to him not just on a one-to-one basis through prayer, but in Scripture stories, community experiences, Church teaching, and spiritual directors. Ignatius humbly *trusted* that God reveals his will for us through a number of instruments and channels. Following these same lines, the movement fostered by the *Spiritual Exercises* is not just about our personal relationship with Jesus. Rather, it fundamentally involves fostering the kingdom of God in the world. Remarkably, in order for the kingdom of God to be ushered into the world, God requires us, that is, our cooperation. Remember that the first action taken by Jesus in bringing about this new reality was to call his disciples by the water. In this calling, Christ expands our hearts with grace, giving us the desire and generosity to respond with him in addressing this disordered universe. We, as a community of disciples, are thus essential to God's redemptive work.

Since Christ does not simply want to save us as individual persons but also calls us to join the struggle to save the world, our vocation—our divine calling—must be about more than simply my needs, my preferences, my wishes. Instead, as Frederick Buechner so rightly defined it, our vocation is this: "The place God calls you to is the place where your deep gladness and the world's deep hunger meet" (Buechner, *Wishful Thinking*, 95). This makes eminent sense, for God's will for us is to live in love, and love always involves taking us to the edges of ourselves to more fully give ourselves to the other and to the world.

Pacing Scout

Scout awakens from her nap and resumes her pacing on the packs. She takes an intense interest in the water, leaning over and sniffing it. She then reaches out a paw and touches it. She begins to paw it, almost as if she is trying to help us paddle the canoe. "Hey,

Ian," I yell, "Take a look at Scout. She must see what we are doing and she's trying to imitate us!" Ian turns and looks. We chuckle at her ineffective but endearing antics.

Then I notice that she is still trying to sniff the water...and suddenly I reframe my interpretation of her behavior based on past observations. "Er, Ian," I state quickly, "Let's head to shore. Maybe Scout needs to go to the bathroom." There is an island straight ahead, so we start paddling for it. At the same time, Scout abandons her investigations of the water and begins to sniff around our packs. Now *I* am getting nervous. We are only ten yards from the beach when Scout squats and urinates on Ian's bag. The packs are waterproof, but all the same Ian moans, "Why did she have to pick out my bag!?! Why not your pack?"

We run the canoe aground and pull Scout ashore. Ian immediately grabs his bag and repeatedly dunks its top into the water. We decide to unload the canoe so that we can wash it. In the meantime, Scout is having a grand time tearing around the island, chasing birds, and smelling every object. It's about noon, so we transform this emergency landing into our lunchtime stopover. Ian joins Scout's fun by chasing her and being chased along the long sandy beach. He takes out her ball and tries to engage her in a game of fetch—the purpose of which she hasn't quite mastered, as she rarely returns with the ball.

Over lunch, Ian and I laugh as we revel in "The Scout Incident." The island lunch and the shared humor reminds me of the "snake on the log" misadventure with David. David and I regaled family and friends with our saga about the "Golf Net Tent Fiasco," but I realize that we never shared the snake incident. So I tell Ian all about it, chuckling heartily as I describe us scrambling away when the snake suddenly moved after David firmly hit the log with the folding chair.

Ian looks at me with wide-eyed surprise. Just as he did when I told him that still water runs deep, he looks incredulously at me. "Why the heck did you tell David to do that? Why didn't you just get into the canoe and leave without disturbing it?" But this time, his skepticism is wiser. I lamely say, "I don't know. We were curious. We weren't considering the consequences." Now a deadpan smile replaces Ian's dubious expression, as he says, "Now, Dad, let's make good choices." He hoots, knowing that I get the point: he is mockingly reproducing one of my pet mantras that the boys have heard me direct innumerable times at them.

I am speechless. He is right. I did make some foolish choices in that situation. There's a Scripture text I printed on a card long ago to carry in my wallet: "For we are what he has made us, created in Christ Jesus for good works, which God prepared beforehand to be our way of life" (Ephesians 2:10). When it came to that snake, I had veered off from that purpose a bit.

The power of this biblical text, however, became clear to me five years ago when my wife and I decided to tackle a house-keeping chore we had put off for years. The job: organizing our children's art projects, report cards, homework papers, and sports memorabilia. These precious pieces of the past were mixed together in overflowing, dilapidated cardboard boxes. So we bought four large plastic storage containers—one for each of our four sons—and then spent a somewhat misty-eyed afternoon sorting these mementos.

When we finished, it struck us that only a foot of space was left in Ian's box and even less in our older boys' boxes. My wife turned to me and said, "We don't have much time left to fill up these boxes of memories that will have to equip our sons for life. We need to think about the skills that we still have to teach them before they head off on their own to college." So we made a list: learn how to sew a hem and button, change the car's oil, balance a checkbook, and many other tasks about as mundane as the countless math worksheets with bright red stars that we had just carefully stored in their boxes.

As time passed, it became clear that one more crucial skill needed to be added: the tools to discern God's will in one's life. We rarely face decisions between a known good and an obvious evil. And even if we do, that is not a matter for discernment.

Rather, it is a matter of resolve—that is, mustering up the courage to choose the right thing.

Everyday life, though, is filled mostly with choices between two goods: Do I stay late at work so that I am able to better support my family financially, or do I leave early so I can deepen my relationship with my children and spouse? Do I say "yes" to a request to help at a church function that will enhance the community's spirit, or do I say "no" so that I can spend an afternoon recharging my personal batteries so I will be more patient with others? How do we determine which specific good is God's will?

Happily, the great spiritual masters in our tradition, especially Saint Ignatius, have provided some guidance. Building on his insight about how God speaks to us through our affective response to choices (the spirits of consolation and desolation), Ignatius developed certain prayer techniques that we can use to choose the more loving way. These prayer methods are just different ways of asking the second God Question, but their genius is that we imaginatively *encounter* the question of who God is calling us to be through actual experiences of consolation and desolation, which are made real through prayer.

At various crucial points in their lives, my wife and I offered our sons the following five Ignatian-inspired methods of prayerfully discerning a choice:

1. *Imaginatively Living With a Decision.* Wake up one morning pretending that you have made "Choice A" and experience the day in light of this decision. Pay particular attention on how you feel (i.e., consoled or desolate) in light of this decision. Note how it affects your relationships and interactions with others. The next morning, repeat this exercise, but pretending that you have made "Choice B." In prayer, weigh these two different choices in light of your experience of these two days.

2. *Talking With a Stranger.* If I were to listen to a stranger facing this same decision—one who was in the same life cir-

cumstances and for whom I wanted the best and most loving life—what would I tell him or her?

3. *Reflecting From My Deathbed.* If I were old and dying and could think back with clarity on all the choices of my life, what decision would I wish I had made right now?

4. *Conversing With Jesus.* After my life has ended and I talk with Jesus about what it has meant, what would give him the most joy to hear me say about this particular choice?

5. *Weighing the Bonds of Friendship.* Which of my options seems to bring me closer to God, and which separates me from my friendship with God by binding me to unhealthy things (prestige, need for appreciation, fear of the future, and so on)?

Boxes. Plans. Decisions. Dreams. When I first jotted down that quote from Ephesians (Ephesians 2:10), I saw it as an indictment: that I had better make sure I was living up to God's expectations. God's will, though, is not about some sort of performance evaluation, but rather it is more like an invitation to live love vigorously. Hence, the point of a box of paper memories is not to fill it, as my wife and I once thought, but to transform it day after day into the kindling that enflames the fire of God's passionate love within us. Let's light some bonfires!

Burning Fire

Which is exactly what Ian and I do that night. Once we set off from our lunch, we only go a few miles farther down the river before I decide it is prudent to select a campsite for the night. The skies are still sketchy with rain. The maps show that we will be entering a stretch of the river with few islands. Properly chastised for my lack of prudence during the snake encounter, I decide that we will set up camp so that we don't get stuck in this approaching "no-man's land" during a thunderstorm. So just past Lone Rock, we select a large sand island for our campsite.

This island has the benefit of a sizeable snag of dead trees and branches, so we have plenty of fuel for a brilliant campfire. We set up camp and then enjoy a late afternoon consisting of fishing, playing catch with a football, and having fun as we watch Scout's antics. After dinner, we do indeed build a great fire and enjoy roasting marshmallows for s'mores. The flickering flames are somewhat hypnotic, especially on this pitch-dark night. Huddled around the fire's warmth and enchantment, we get caught up in conversation as we stare into its mesmerizing blaze.

The spell is broken when Ian suddenly asked, "Where's Scout?" Sure enough, she has wandered away from the fire's glowing ring. We shout her name. Nothing emerges from the impenetrable darkness. We shout again and listen. We hear no rustling of her footsteps or jingling of her collar tags. We call one more time. She does not return. But that is no big surprise; as the morning has testified, coming on command is not Scout's particular talent.

We begin to search the island for her. We have little hope of seeing her without a flashlight, as her black coat effectively hides her presence in the murky darkness. So we sweep our flashlights across the sandy surface as we walk. We thoroughly search the entire island. No luck. With every step, Ian is growing increasingly agitated. We work our way back to our starting point when Ian's beam picks up two iridescent eyes, glowing in the darkness. There is Scout, just yards from our tent, curled up and comfortable but with her head alert. She had been there the whole time!

We decide to be safe and tie a tethered rope to Scout's collar for the night. We return to the fire. Anxious to relieve the stress of the recent experience, I say to Ian, "Did you hear about the dyslexic, insomniac, agnostic?" Ian, knowing a joke is coming, responds warily, "No." I deliver the punch line: "He stayed up all night wondering if there really was a dog." Ian stares at me blankly. "I don't get it. What's a dysle... whatever." I then have to explain the meaning of each word. After the vocabulary lesson, Ian just rolls his eyes and says, "Oh."

With that, we call it a night. As we lie in our sleeping bags, I hear Ian's rhythmic breathing as he falls asleep. The sound of his breaths merges with the babbling water of the passing river. I recall my efforts that day to teach Ian about the ways of the river until I too, merge my breathing with the river's journey.

Entering Prayer

There is a parable about another young person's lessons from the river. Upon arrival at the monastery, a new monk saw a saintly old monk, deep in pray next to a river. The young monk approached him and asked, "Teach me to pray." The old monk stared intently at him a moment, then grabbed him by the hair and plunged his head under the water, holding it there. When the panicking young man finally broke loose, he sputtered "Why did you do that?" The old monk responded, "I just gave you your first lesson in prayer: you must desire to pray as badly as you just now wanted to breathe if you truly want to love God."

This story epitomizes Ignatius' sense of the place of prayer in our journey to cleaving ourselves to Jesus Christ. We already have discovered the first step in love is *desire*. We all know this from our human relationships. If my desires had not initially attracted me to my wife...well, then I would not be enfolded today within our sustaining, ever-expanding love relationship. But attraction must move to relationship, to loving the *real* person. I find that I love better when I love my *wife* rather than my *idea* of my wife—that is, loving her as I encounter her in the everyday-ness of life.

Given how hard it is to love the people we see, hear, and touch every day, we face a true challenge when it comes to God: how do we love an "invisible" God? Of course, we are privileged to touch God in the sacraments, but when reading Scripture, it is easy to feel as if we are observing Jesus from a distance. We *hear* about Jesus; we are not there ourselves conversing with him, laughing with him, crying with him. We tend to comprehend only the spiritualized "idea" of Jesus, not to experience a real encounter with the flesh-and-blood person of Jesus.

Here Ignatius would stop us and say: "What do you mean you can't really be there with Jesus? Yes, you can: through the power of a prayerful imagination and the portal of Scripture!" Ignatius suggests that we, through the "application of the senses," can overcome this barrier by using our imagination to place ourselves inside the gospel stories. Specifically, we are to assume the role of a particular character in the story (a disciple, a bystander, a person seeking a cure) and experience the events through that person.

To make the scene become real, Ignatius recommends that we feel ourselves as physically and tangibly present as possible in that scene. For example, smell the foods if the story takes place during a meal, taste the dust in your mouth if it involves walking along a roadway, feel the rough-hewn stone if leaning against a wall, see the scene from the color of the trees to the wrinkles in people's faces, hear every inflection as someone is speaking and the random comments of the bystanders. The point is to use the imagination to re-create a sensory experience of the biblical passage to close the historical distance and then let the scene unfold as "live action." Often referred to as Ignatian contemplation or guided imagery, the goal of this type of prayer is to experience an event in Jesus' life by composing the scene with as much detail and sensory information as possible.

Ignatian contemplation follows these steps:

1. *Choosing a Scripture passage and reading it thoroughly.* Select or create a character you will be in the story.
2. *Settling yourself.* Offer a prayer of thanksgiving for this moment, and ask for the grace you seek.
3. *Imagining the gospel scene by placing yourself in it.* Use your imagination to *feel* the scene with your senses as if you were actually there. Notice not only what is said, but what people *do*—their actions. Let the scene unfold as you re-

member it from your reading, and do not fret if you do not remember every word or action. Trust the Spirit to allow you to recall those details essential for your prayer. In fact, you should feel free to add actions and conversations to the story, allowing God's spirit to speak to you through your active imagination. One caution: this is *not* like watching a movie. Instead, you are a full participant directly engaged with the emerging action.

4. *Ending with a conversation with God the Father, Christ, the Holy Spirit, or one of the saints, such as Mary.* Make sure you both speak and listen as you reflect on what you now know more fully about this person named Jesus after this encounter.

5. *After thanking God for this grace, saying an Our Father.*

The purpose is to use Scripture and our imaginations to encounter Jesus Christ in *his* everyday life. This lets us move from *longing* to *love* as we use our imaginations to see, hear, touch, and walk with Jesus. Thus the goal is not to decide "What would Jesus do?" (WWJD) but to experience "What is Jesus doing?" (WIJD) so that we can enter into relationship with Jesus as we encounter Jesus' life "firsthand" through our imaginations.

Ignatius offers this method of prayer so that we don't just admire Jesus, nor just obey Jesus, nor just imitate Jesus. Rather Ignatius' ultimate goal is to achieve what Ronald Rolheiser calls "undergoing Jesus" (Rolheiser, *The Holy Longing*, 74–81). By praying in this active fashion with our imaginations, we "absorb" Jesus, just as we in some form or fashion absorb within us everyone else whom we love intensely. In this manner, Jesus' way of reacting and treating others becomes *our* way of responding in our own lives because we have internalized his way of being by journeying completely with him. "Undergoing Jesus" means becoming God's skin on earth by being part of the Body of Christ. As the Body of Christ, God's Incarnation continues today on the earth in part through us.

A parable may clarify this point. Hands...he was missing his hands! Years ago, someone vandalized a statue in a Catholic church by breaking off the hands of Jesus' outstretched arms. The congregation was devastated. However, as they contemplated ways to fix it, they suddenly realized that this broken statue said something rather profound about our faith. They decided not to replace the stone hands, but instead placed a plaque before it that read: "I have no hands but yours." The parishioners were adapting a longer saying from Saint Teresa of Ávila: "Christ has no body now on earth but yours, no hands but yours, no feet but yours. Yours are the eyes through which Christ's compassion looks out on the world, yours are the feet with which He is to go about doing good. Yours are the hands with which He is to bless us now."

I once related this story during dinner to make a point about the purpose of the Lenten season. Ian had a self-satisfied smile when he chimed in, "So you're saying we are supposed to 'lend' a hand for *Lent!*" Later that night, my wife was staring at her own hands. She remarked, "You know, as I get older I'm noticing that my hands are starting to look more and more like my grandmother's hands. It's a little distressing." However, maybe the real issue is whether our hands, over the course of our lives, start looking more and more to us like Jesus' hands. If they don't, then that's *really* disturbing. Paul said something similar when he wrote that we are "a letter of Christ...written not with ink but with the Spirit of the Living God, not on tablets of stone but on tablets of human hearts" (2 Corinthians 3:3). We are all called to be Christ's hands in the world—not hands of stone, but heart-inspired hands of flesh that comfort, heal, and love.

Since he was a Jesuit, I suppose that, as Marquette lay almost 350 years earlier on a sandbar island much like this one, he prayed with some Scripture passage in the active, imaginative manner promoted by Ignatius. Maybe by the flickering flames of a dying fire, he read the story of Jesus' baptism and then re-experienced it in prayer, hearing first-hand as God uttered that tender name for the Son. On some deep level, that prayer must have invariably seeped into his very pores so that Christ's very mind informed Marquette's choices and actions in the world. I wonder if Ignatius heard Christ's voice rising from the deep, dark stillness, calling him forward to follow him in ushering in the kingdom of God. Maybe Ignatius clasped his hands over his face in awe, and then... as he slowly lowered them...he saw in the embers' glow the shape and texture of Jesus' own hands within his own. If so, then I wonder if he then whispered to himself, "There really is a God!"

Flying Lessons

The clouds departed with the night, and the sun's sparkling rays are dancing on the river's waters the next morning. It stays cool, which makes for easier paddling but prevents us from swimming. All in all, it is going to be a great day.

We pack up and load the canoe. Scout climbs atop the packs by her own volition. She now feels quite comfortable riding in the canoe and looks excited about getting under way. Quite a change from yesterday.

We haven't journeyed far down the river when a small aircraft, flying low, appears. It is obviously following the line of the river, and I assume the passengers are taking in the river's beautiful scenery. My reading about the river over the past few weeks has made me a fount of interesting anecdotes about the historical happenings in the Driftless Area. So, after the plane passes, I tell Ian the story of Doctor Bertha Reynolds, who set up shop in the town of Lone Rock in 1902.

A female doctor in the early years of the twentieth century is notable enough, but she became known during her forty-one-year career for her courage and dedication. Living when there was no bridge over this section of the river, many are the stories of her willingness to scamper across the river's thin and treacherous spring ice to respond quickly to a sick call. Even in the worst weather, she journeyed by foot, horse, and later car along mud-slick and snow-packed roads that others claimed were impassable.

Nothing would stop her from responding to an appeal for healing help until one particularly violent spring thaw. She got a call from across the river, but the torrent of rushing waters from the winter melt made crossing the river impossible, even for this intrepid soul. As luck would have it, though, a young barnstorming pilot had flown into Lone Rock the previous day. She sent a messenger, asking if he would fly her to the other side of the river so that she could respond to this medical emergency. The pilot agreed, telling her to meet him at his airplane. As she climbed into the cockpit, she warmly asked, "What's your name, young man?" The response she heard was just a name, an ordinary name. It would be years later that the name took on new significance. "Charles Lindbergh," the baby-faced pilot answered. And, as the saying goes, the rest is history.

Could it be that encounters with plucky, barrier-breaking people like Dr. Reynolds led Lindbergh to hear himself called by a new name: "My Intrepid One, go and shrink the distance between the Old and New by flying the sea." That famous flight brought him great acclaim, but Lindbergh's later anti-Semitic comments transform his story into a cautionary tale. Discernment is not a one-time event, but an ongoing process, the validity of which must always be measured by the standard of love.

There is something about adventurers that attracts the imagination of a young teenager, as I find out as Ian and I talk of many things as we paddle down the river. I start probing his "favorites": favorite friend, favorite athlete, favorite book, and so on. He recently has seen *Lawrence of Arabia* for the first time, so I am not surprised when this is listed as his favorite movie. All the same, I have to smile at this answer, but my smile has nothing to do with Ian. Rather, it has to do with a connection between this movie and a case of "mistaken identity" that I heard when I was teaching at a liberal arts college. During one of the faculty development sessions, we were asked to talk in small groups about how education can transform lives. One of our colleagues, an English professor, told a story that she said was infamous at the institution where she had done her graduate work.

As the story goes, a business student, who needed to fulfill his English requirement, registered for a course entitled "The Writings of D. H. Lawrence" because he had really liked the movie *Lawrence of Arabia.* When he showed up on the first day of class, he quickly realized his error. To his dismay, the Lawrence who was the subject of this class was not the swash-buckling World War I war hero, but a poet!

He was going to drop the course, but then he observed that he was the only male in a classroom full of attractive female students (we've got desire working here!). While he decided to stay in the course, he wasn't going to waste his beer money on an expensive poetry book. So he bought the required text at a local used bookstore. As he thumbed through the book, he was surprised to discover that the poetry was very sensual stuff. Further, he noticed that the book's previous owner had underlined some of the most erotic lines and had written comments in the margins next to the more provocative sections. Then he noticed one more thing: the previous owner's name and phone number were listed on the inside cover—and it was a woman's name.

Over the course of the semester, this young man wondered about this mystery woman whose name was emblazoned on the front cover. The more he noticed what caught her attention in Lawrence's poetry, the more he speculated about her. Finally, his curiosity got the best of him. He decided to call her. Anticipating that the former owner was a student at his college who had taken this course the previous semester, you can imagine his surprise when the woman who answered "yes" when he asked for her by name was a seventy-five-year-old grandmother who had been a high-school English teacher. Evidently, she had recently moved into a small assisted-living apartment and had disposed of her rather large book collection.

Of course, the young man had to cover up his real motivations for calling. He professed a great admiration for Lawrence's poetry and said he called her because he could see by her margin notes that she loved Lawrence, too. She invited him to come talk about Lawrence's writings. Too embarrassed to do otherwise, he agreed. As they talked, Lawrence's poetry came alive for this young man. She invited him back and they soon formed a friendly relationship that lasted through his college years.

That's a great story. It tells us that our desires are a mysterious force that will take us to places we never expect or anticipate— they take us beyond ourselves. God calls us through the dreams that arise from our desires. For this reason, it is no surprise that in the Gospel of John, Jesus begins forming his church by gathering disciples through this question: What are you seeking? However, the call of discipleship will always take us out of our comfort zones; it will stretch us because God's kingdom draws us into the frightening, wonderful immensity of life.

So we—the Church—are those called through our desires to cross thresholds into the unknown, as did that business student, Charles Lindbergh, Marquette, and Ignatius. That is what we are to do.

Crossing Thresholds

Marquette left us a written record of his own moment of fearful decision as he stood on the cusp of realizing his greatest dream. As his expedition traveled down the Wisconsin River and the first three hundred miles down the Mississippi, they did not encounter a single Native American. Part of this was by design, for they were terrified about stumbling upon hostile tribes. So they took many precautions: lighting small cooking fires, sleeping in the canoes anchored in the middle of the river, maintaining a sentry every night. But Marquette's dream, which he had prayerfully discerned by the spirits of consolation and desolation, was not to hide from the Native American tribes but to befriend them so that he might share with them the gift of Christ's love.

Then on June 25, Marquette was confronted with the scary reality of his call. On that day, they found human footprints pressed within the muddy shore and a beaten path through a meadow. They rightly guessed that the trail would lead to an Indian village. But would they find there the Illinois, whose tongue Marquette had diligently learned in preparation for this monumental encounter? Even if it was an Illinois village, would they wait to hear Marquette's soothing words, or would they be so startled by these strangers that they would attack at first sight? Or did this trail lead to the village of a totally different tribe, maybe even the Lakota, whom the other tribes told Jolliet and Marquette would kill anyone they found in their territory?

The moment of decision had arrived for Marquette. I wonder what made him go forward. Was it simply shame and embarrassment if the rugged men of the band saw him retreat in fear? Was it the power of the First Principle and Foundation, which had inculcated within him an active sense of indifference because God is in all things? Was it because he properly placed himself in the world—in which he simultaneously knew his existence to be dreadfully insignificant and wondrously grand—so that he saw all of life within the context of gratitude? Was he equipped to respond with openness to this challenge because of the reflective spirit developed within him by his daily practice of the Examen? Was it because God had been calling him by name through his desires for this very moment? Was it the years of discerning the spirits of consolation and desolation that prepared him to walk into God's joy, regardless of the cost? Was it that he quickly prayed with one of Ignatius' ways of considering a choice, which led him to come *into* his decision? Was it that he had absorbed the sacrificing love of Christ through his constant prayer with

Scripture by means of Ignatian contemplation, with its application of the senses? Or was it all of these things that formed a way of being within him?

We will never know. But we do know this: he and Jolliet stepped forward on this path. This is Marquette's account from his journal of this weighty decision:

> We left our two canoes under the guard of our people, strictly charging them not to allow themselves to be taken by surprise, and then Monsieur Jolliet and I set off on a rather dangerous mission for two men who exposed themselves, alone, to the mercy of a barbarous and unknown people. We silently followed the narrow path, and after walking about two leagues [six miles], we discovered a village on the bank of a river and two others on a hill distant about half a league from the first. At this point, we heartily commended ourselves to God, and after imploring his aid, we went on, but no one noticed us. We approached so near that we could even hear the Indians talking. We therefore decided that it was time to reveal ourselves. Stopping and advancing no further [sic], we began to yell as loudly as we could. (*JR*, 196)

I find it interesting that both Marquette and Jolliet went forward. Wouldn't it have been more logical for one of these leaders to stay behind with the canoe's guard party in the fear that this advance party might not return alive? The two of them were essential to this expedition's commission, since only they knew how to record the instrument readings that were vital to establishing the French claims upon this new territory. If the plan was to scamper back to French territory if disaster struck, wouldn't it have made more sense to take a few more men with them—or maybe even the entire band—in case they did indeed run into trouble? So I wonder if the truth of the matter is that the other men simply refused, out of fear, to follow.

If this is the case, is it just happenstance that Jolliet had also been foundationally formed by Ignatian spirituality? As a young man, he too had been a Jesuit for five years until he left the seminary when he realized that God was not calling him to religious life. So both of these men, Jolliet and Marquette, were bonded to Christ through the First Principle and Foundation, the daily Examen, and the other methods of Ignatian prayer.

Mark Link says that Christians can be described as one of the following types of boats: rafts, sailboats, or tugboats. The *rafts* are passive Christians who follow Jesus only because some external force is pushing or pulling them along, but they really aren't intentionally or purposefully living the Christian life. *Sailboat* Christians only follow Jesus in sunny weather when there is a favorable breeze. But when the storm starts brewing, they inevitably abandon the direction of Jesus because their course is determined by the whipping winds and swamping waves. In other words, they follow Jesus as long as there is no cost or sacrifice involved with living a faithful life. *Tugboats*, however, push themselves forward, regardless of the circumstances of the weather or cost, to follow Jesus. They may not travel very fast, but they always move in the direction of Jesus so that they might join his purposeful work of moving all the ships to safe harbor (see Link, *Challenge* [1993], 236).

Link's metaphor alludes to what Ignatius describes as "Three Types of People" in the *Spiritual Exercises*. The goal, of course, is to become like "tugboats" as in Link's analogy. But we can only do this by developing an intense loyalty to and love of Christ by walking in prayer with Jesus. As a result of this direct prayerful encounter with Jesus, the person is invariably called to reflect on three key questions, which Ignatius puts at the center of the *Spiritual Exercises:*

- What have I done for Christ?
- What am I doing for Christ?
- What will I do for Christ?

If we are truly free by living in the love of God, Ignatius was sure that we would be stretched and taken to new vistas of existence. Fully encountering God invariably not only changes us, but also leads us to love better. God's love takes us across new thresholds in our lives; it draws us to that next, deeper step of love. Specifically, encountering Christ leads us to ask these questions: how has and is God making me and, in light of that encounter, how do I need to reformulate my life to be a more faithful follower of Christ?

If I look at the names that I use for Jesus, I realize that I mainly use "sailboat" names: Teacher, Friend, Brother. I rarely use "tugboat" names for Jesus in my prayer: Suffering Messiah, Crucified Lord, Sacrificed Son. These terms are not as warm and comforting as "sailboat" names. Disturbing questions and perplexing paradox lie within the tugboat names. If Christ suffered, am I called to suffer as his disciple? How is one both Lord and crucified? Is God in the pain of life as much as in the joy of being? These questions run deep within the river's current, and they push us into the edgy reality of fearful paths. If I am honest with myself, I too would have stayed with those men guarding the familiar canoes.

So what happened after our two disciples called out to the Indian village?

> On hearing the shout, the Indians quickly issued from their cabins, and having probably recognized us as Frenchmen, especially when they saw a black robe—or, at least, having no cause for distrust, as we were only two men and had given them notice of our arrival— they appointed four old men to come and speak to us.... [W]hen they had drawn near, they stopped to look at us attentively....I therefore spoke to them first, asking them who they were. They replied that they were Illinois, and as a token of peace, they offered us their pipes to smoke. (*JR*, 196–197)

Marquette's narrative continues at great length in describing this first encounter. Although their visit with these people of the Illinois tribe only lasted two days, it is the longest section of Marquette's diary. In fact, all of Marquette's descriptions of the landscape they passed are rather brief, but his accounts of interactions with native peoples are extensive. Maybe that is not surprising, given that Marquette undertook this journey out of a call to form a relationship with the people of the river, not to discover a new land. His call came from relationship with Christ, which in turn drew him out into a relationship with the stranger.

Calling Eagles

Ian and I spend a pleasant and rewarding day as we continue down the river. Approaching the Avoca State Wildlife area, which is the largest tall-grass prairie east of the Mississippi, we encounter a plethora of water fowl: blue herons, ducks, cranes, and many other types of birds. Our excitement over seeing bald eagles soaring high overhead turns into elation when a bald eagle swoops down to tree level and follows the river's line as it, with keen eye, searches for unsuspecting fish. Adding to the thrill is the experience of drifting under a tree housing a solitary roosting eagle that suddenly gives out a piercing call to a mate. Magnificent!

After a full day of steady paddling, we reach our takeout location: Muscoda. The town supports a nice park along the river's edge. After we beach the canoe, I stretch out on a picnic bench to await the arrival of my wife, Stephanie, who is chauffeuring our third-oldest son, Micah, to this meeting spot. Ian and Micah will switch places, and Micah and I will continue down the river for the third leg of the Russell River Rendezvous.

As we await Steph and Micah's arrival, Ian amuses himself by trying to perfect his rock-skipping ability. His success is minimal; rocks aren't meant to travel on the river. Scout is dashing madly up and down the shore, looking for adventure. Soon, I hear Ian yelling, "Come here, Scout. Come! Here you go, girl. Scout! Come *here!*" I look up to see Ian running after Scout, who is far upriver. Scout looks up, sees Ian running toward him, and then dashes ten yards farther upriver. Scout pauses, again peeking back at Ian. This time, Ian stops, turns and runs downriver. Scout watches Ian for a moment and then begins to give wild chase. I smile. Same old Scout!

I return to my ruminations about the true meaning of this river's name. Then, I stop. Scout and I aren't that different. I spend most of my life randomly dashing on the shore too—and my interest in following God's call is about as fickle. Only when I am afraid of being desperately left alone (usually due to life's pain or my sin) do I hear God beckoning me to continue down the river.

Here, though, is the good news: God meets us where we are, even if we are perched on a lonely rock. Such was the case with three of the disciples. According to Luke's account of the transfiguration (see 9:28–36), they were asleep on a mountain top when they awoke to see the transfigured form of Jesus with Moses and Elijah. True to his name, Peter gave a "rock" answer to this mystical experience: let's build booths right here and live on stone. Peter is off beam once again because he posed an answer without even considering the question. God doesn't shake Peter by his lapels, shouting, "What is wrong with you?" Instead, Luke tells us that God enfolds them within a cloud—within vaporized water—and says, "This is my Son, my Chosen; listen to him!" Much like at Jesus' baptism scene, God the Father reveals one of God's names for Jesus: Chosen Son. Now, however, this name is not revealed in order to call forth Jesus, but his disciples...and us.

Interestingly, just before the transfiguration story Jesus tells his disciples that he will suffer and that those who will follow him will also need to take up their cross (see Luke 9:22–27), which is a lesson that Peter utterly rejects, according to Mark (8:31–33) and Matthew (16:21–23). Nonetheless, our loving God does not write Peter off but rather brings the river's water to his craggy roost. God roots out Peter's fear by continuing to encounter him even as he clings to rock and to call him forth by revealing to him one of the Father's tender terms for Jesus. This, however, is not a sailboat name, but a tugboat one, for Jesus is chosen to die on a cross as an end result of God's outpouring love for the world. With that name, "Chosen One," God challenges and prepares Peter for the hard fact of Jesus' impending death, as well as the sacrifices of discipleship. So I wonder if Peter, on hearing Jesus' name, did not also hear something new in his own: "Rocky, let go and plunge into the awe-full Mystery."

So, does it really matter if the name for this river originally meant "River through the Red Rock" or "The Gathering of Waters"? Whatever the river's name, God meets us wherever we are: on the hard shore or the flowing water. In that place, God names our experience to call us into the Immense Waters. Living in the second God Question means being named what we are—and hearing God call us forth through our wondrous desires, our prayerful encounters with Christ, and our discernment of the spirits of consolation and desolation into our vocation, our mission. I smile, lie down again on the bench, listening for the river's watery whispering of names.

CHAPTER THREE

How Is God Caring for Us?

What is our place in the world?
Who is God calling us to be?
How is God caring for us?
Where is God's love?

Night Laughter

The grave voice reverberates in the night air: "Hundreds of years ago, rugged men went out in the vast wilderness of early America with a great dream in their minds, vision in their eyes, and big nine-pound hammers clasped in their hands. These men of yesteryear were building an immense spider web of steel rails spanning the width and breadth of the country. Toiling and inching their way across the vast bosom of America....Thought I'd throw a little sex in the show." Laughter bursts forth from the radio, joining our own.

My sixteen-year-old and third-oldest son, Micah, and I are camped on an island just a stone's throw downriver from Muscoda. Earlier that day, road construction had considerably delayed Micah and my wife's arrival at Muscoda, where Ian and I were waiting so the two boys could switch places. Scout was also going back with Ian and Steph. Once my wife arrived, we had to shuttle the other car from the Spring Green put-in site down to Boscobel, which is the takeout location for this third leg of the trip with Micah. This shuttling process took much longer than I had anticipated.

By the time we got back to Muscoda, a gorgeous sunset, dominated by brilliant streaks of orange, framed our canoe as Micah and I shoved off into water that was rapidly and ominously taking on the dark character of the approaching night. Stopping at the first island we reached, we set up our camp. My joke to Micah, "There's nothing like pitching camp in pitch darkness!" didn't lift the gloominess of this untidy night. Since we wouldn't share the enjoyment of a campfire because we hadn't had time to find firewood, I tried to salvage the evening by firing up our nifty propane backpacking stove so that we could roast marsh-mallows and make s'mores. Unfortunately, water had gotten into the marshmallow bag, creating a gooey white glob.

So there we sat in the dark, eating dry chocolate between two uninspiring graham crackers. I decided to break the "no-electronic-devices rule" that I had instituted for this trip. I pulled out the emergency radio—one that you charge by frantically turning a hand crank for a few minutes—and fortuitously found a station broadcasting a Smothers Brothers comedy show.

As the laughter subsides, the serious Smothers brother, Dick, chastises Tommy for that last innuendo, telling him to get back on track. So Tommy continues, "All right. But this wasn't just a fun job. [More laughter.] Wherever these railroad men went, there lurked dangers. Some of the railroad men would get nervous at night and they would jump out of bed and say, 'Hey, I saw a danger lurk!' There was lurking in the mountains, and they had to build bridges across raging deserts and blazing rivers."

Dick interjects, "Tommy, raging deserts and blazing rivers?" Oblivious, Tommy resumes his tale, "And these railroad men, they were fearless, and they had to build railroad bridges that spanned deep crevasses with big railroad pretzels. And oftentimes at the bottom of these crevasses, there lurked pewmas. Vicious pewmas. The railroad men would say, 'Wow, look at those pewmas down there in the crevasses.'"

Incredulous over the malapropisms, Dick spews, "Pewmas?! That's wrong! There weren't any *pumas* in the crevasses, Tommy, because there aren't any pumas in this country. There are no pumas in America. Do you want to keep your story historically correct? Then get rid of the pumas right now." A quieter Tommy continues, "Well, there were these vicious beasts in these crevasses. And these railroad men were so afraid. And these railroad men came up to these crevasses and said, 'Wow, look at those vicious beasts in the crevasses...Pew, they sure smell like pewmas!'"

Our laughter briefly pushes back the night's darkness, so that a glow of shared companionship radiates in this sandy space. We listen to the rest of the comedy show and then some music but don't bother cranking up the radio again when its power slowly ebbs away. Instead, we keep talking in the darkness, which now seems like a warm blanket wrapped around us.

While there are many ways that one might answer the third God Question—*How is God caring for us?*—surely God's gift of human laughter is matchless in transforming dejection into solace. I used to assume that the words *humor* and *human* derived from the same Latin root, *humus*, which means dirt, earth. Thus, humor "works" because it reminds us of the curious limitations of our humanity. I made mention of this "insight" to a friend of mine who is a serious student of Latin. He chuckled (appropriately) and said that, while human comes from *humus*, humor comes from a different Latin word, *umor*, which means moisture, fluid, or vapor. It's the same Latin root for our English word *humidity*. He then drolly added that my theory was thus "all wet."

Even better! Humor is the result of mixing our watery essence with our earthly natures, thus reminding us that we dirt-beings belong in the river, that humor, in a way, dissolves us in the river. Within humor is the knowledge of life's irony: we most become who we are when we allow ourselves to be rendered into what we are not. After all, the premise underlying every funny joke, sarcastic remark, and pitiful pun is the incongruence between what is and what should be. Humor, then, is the art of paradox. Humor pushes off the shore and into the river.

Night Terror

During this night conversation, I cautiously venture into a new topic, "Well, this night is a lot calmer than the last time we camped together on the Wisconsin." Micah responds, "What do you mean?" I am surprised by the question. "Don't you remember that ferocious thunderstorm on our last canoe trip down this river?" Micah answers, "Oh, yeah. Sure, I remember some things."

I am predisposed to think out loud, verbalizing my every thought, rambling on as I try to clarify my own mind. But not Micah. He is more introspective and thoughtful. He is certainly a good communicator, but he is not one to run at the mouth. When he was a baby learning to speak, we worried when he suddenly stopped repeating words to us. You know the drill. The parent says "ball" and the child replies, "ball." Micah just stopped doing that, regardless of the amount of prompting offered. We were obviously concerned, but the doctor said there was nothing physically wrong. Then, one day Micah started speaking again—in complete sentences. Not just subject-verb sentences, but subject-verb-direct object-prepositional phrase sentences! It was almost as if he had decided not to speak until he had figured out how this whole communication thing worked. He just observed, soaked it in, and then spoke when he was ready to do it completely. That trait remains in Micah. He listens first and speaks only when he has figured out his thoughts.

There is silence for a while. Micah is renowned among our sons for his memory. We can be talking about some past vacation or family event, and Micah will recall detail after detail, things that the rest of us have long forgotten.

When I can't wait any longer, I ask, "Well, what do you remember?" "I remember sand in my macaroni and cheese." Confused, I stammer, "What?" Micah connects the dots. "When we were eating in the tent, sand had gotten into our dinner. And I remember the side of the tent was blowing in and you holding it. And I remember that stick. You took a picture the next morning with me pointing at the top of the stick. The rest was under water. I remember that the newspaper said the wind pushed six semi-trucks over. And I remember that, for the rest of that summer, I wanted to go inside whenever it looked like it was going to rain." Now it is my turn to sit silently, pondering.

His recollections stir up within me many thoughts and feelings from that long, terrible night. Five years earlier, when Micah was only eleven years old, I had initiated this same idea of a four-stage canoe trip with each son accompanying me on a different segment of the journey down the Wisconsin. I only did the first leg—with Micah. I aborted the plan after that nightmare.

During the first day and night, the weather was perfect, as it was on the second day. That second night, Micah and I found a fantastic, secluded camping spot on the east side of a thickly wooded island. We pitched our tent on the island's curled-finger sandy peninsula, which arched upriver, creating a deep "back-water" pool. An ideal swimming hole! We spent the afternoon splashing about in the water. Our steep-banked beach was about two feet above the water level, so we had a great time of running and leaping into the water, seeing who could make the largest splash. Micah planted a stick toward the end of the peninsula to mark our "takeoff" spot.

As I was preparing dinner, the warm summer weather quickly and dramatically changed. The wind began to roar from the west, whipping up the sand. Boiling dark clouds quickly extinguished the sun. Barking thunderclaps and snarling lightning flashes yowled all around us. We barely scampered into the tent with our partially prepared dinner before hammering sheets of rain, driving at a sideways angle due to the violent winds, lashed forth from the sky.

We sat eating our semi-warm, sand-seasoned dinner as the storm raged outside. I assumed that it would, like most intense summer storms, pass quickly. Not only did it persist, but the winds also increased in their ferocity. Micah was getting anxious—and rightly so. Trying to minimize his fears, we began to play cards. I tried to deal the cards nonchalantly with one hand as I frantically clutched the poles of the dome tent with the other to prevent it from collapsing around us. There was real reason to worry. As Micah recalled, we learned the next day that this storm's mighty wind shears literally pushed semi-trailer trucks, traveling on the interstate, over on their sides. There were sightings of tornado funnel clouds.

And the rain was indeed torrential. The wind subsided somewhat, but the rain did not. While Micah slept that night, I periodically unzipped the tent's door, waited for a flash of lightning, and then apprehensively peered at the stick that Micah had lodged into the sand toward the peninsula's tip. As the night progressed, the water rose to the stick, then halfway up the stick, and finally over the stick. Our buffer from the river's current was swiftly diminishing.

We were lucky. Fortuitously, our eastside campsite on the heavily treed island somewhat abated the deadly west wind. Fortunately, our tent was about three feet above the river's initial water level. Nevertheless, all that night I wondered how I could protect my son. Stupidly, I had not brought a transistor radio, so I did not have access even to weather information (hence, the reason for carrying the hand-cranked radio on this trip). Cell phones were not as ubiquitous as billfolds in those days (how quickly modern life has changed!), and we did not own one. No one else in the world knew where we were camped, much less were they able to save us. I was alone in this terrifying situation, alone and responsible for my son's life.

I knew it was foolhardy to try to paddle the canoe to shore. The river was such a surging mass that it was apt to capsize our precarious vessel. I considered retreating to the island's trees and lying huddled among them. The wind was so violent that I feared the sand-rooted trees might very well topple on us. If they didn't, the trees might instead become lightning rods. So there were no good options.

As I listened to my son's vulnerable, even breathing and the ragged howling storm, I realized that I was powerless to protect him from harm. Powerless. All I could do was pray. And hope. Or cry. I prayed. More accurately, I bargained, or at least tried to bargain...with God. I didn't realize it at the time, but I was desperately fumbling to obtain an answer to the third God Question: *How is God caring for us?* In the moments of laughter, the question is a comfort. In times of terror, it becomes an accusation.

Great Wound

We rarely ask the third God Question except when our self-interest is vitally threatened. In these moments of tragedy, though, we phrase the question badly. We ask, "Why is God doing this to me?" Or we don't even ask a question, but simply demand a solution: "Please, Lord, protect me from this disaster." We undoubtedly barter with rather bankrupt chips: "If this terrible thing does not happen, then I promise to_____." And the promise is invariably to become something that we are not or have not been. Desperate resolutions pathetically pushed forward in an attempt to bribe God.

Of the four God Questions, the third is possibly the most difficult for us moderns to ask properly because we are spiritually handicapped by our obsession with avoiding authentic encounters with pain, suffering, and death. Instead, we numb ourselves to its reality by saturating our sensory environment with phony violence on our television shows. We mock it by engaging in adventure activities that are closely choreographed to give the illusion of risk. We marginalize it by hypersecuring our lives behind fences of "perfection" in a delusional effort to eradicate the fear. Ultimately, though, these sham defenses cannot protect us from suffering's veracity.

Direct experiences of our astonishingly absolute human vulnerability come only in flashes, such as when we walk away from a dangerous car accident. Or, it arrives vicariously, such as when airplanes are intentionally flown into ordinary workplace buildings. More profoundly, it shatters our illusions of invincibility when a parent, friend, sibling, or spouse dies.

Even modern Christians are poorly prepared to deal with the third God Question because we mistakenly believe faith should *protect* us from suffering and even death. That concept is the conventional contortion of Christianity. After two thousand years of nailing crucifixes on our household walls, pinning gold crosses on our lapeled chests, and hanging religious medals around our prayerful necks, we still don't "get" the scandalous proclamation of Christianity: God is inextricably intertwined within suffering, and that God is calling us *through* suffering. Not around it, not over it, not under it. *Through* it. We ornament our lives with the image of a crucified man, but we never place its scandalous truth in our hearts.

Not only is the third God Question problematic for twenty-first-century Christians, but it is also the most insuperable question for the age-old religions because the world's pointed pain punctures platitudes about God's care for us. Accordingly, every major world religion offers an explanation for suffering. Some, such as Buddhism, claim that the goal of life is to eliminate suffering by excising its source: our passions and desires. Others, such as Islam, view pain and suffering as directly controlled by Allah, who uses it to test and purify the faith of believers. Suffering is usually accepted within Judaism quite simply as one of the facts of existence whose meaning escapes explanation. These thumbnail descriptions are, of course, generalizations of complex theological theories, but each represents an attempt to answer the third God Question in the face of the reality of human grief.

However, only Christianity has the audacity to respond to the third God Question by placing and keeping suffering front and center by proclaiming that a crucified man is God. No wonder, as Saint Paul noted, the Jews found such talk a stumbling block, and the Gentiles simply poked fun at its foolishness (see 1 Corinthians 1:23). The Lord Almighty of the Universe is ignominiously killed by puny governmental officials in a backwater like Jerusalem? Ridiculous! The Eternal Timeless One has actually and really died a human death on a specific time and date? Impossible! If you think about it practically or philosophically...it just doesn't follow common sense.

Jesus' death *is* rather senseless, but maybe God isn't interested in making sense, but rather in *sensing* our pain. Maybe God is more about entering the paradox of human experience rather than solving it. Or maybe God *is* the paradox—cross *and* resurrection, human *and* divine. Could it be that God simply chose to allow love to trump all theological definitions of the divine? Would God...could God...really love us insignificant humans so much as to participate in our humanity and suffering? The Christian faith emphatically declares *YES!*

That is the central mystery of the Christian faith. God loves us so much that he became human so he could be with us in our pain, even to the point of experiencing our deepest hurt: death. By this act, God did not eliminate suffering here on earth but shares it with us. And in that way, he transforms it. Now the cross makes it crystal clear: nothing can separate us from the love of God—not even death. By messy birth and traumatic death, God has experienced and become the totality of our human reality. So God's salvation plan does not involve us becoming like God, but God becoming us so that we are now like God. God enters all and redeems all.

The irony is that the crucifixion of Jesus (which is intrinsically connected to our belief in the incarnation, resurrection, and the Triune God) is the most distinctive aspect of the Christian message, but we don't teach the profound mystery of the cross. Richard Rohr has gone so far as to call us modern Christians derelict in passing on the faith because we fail to teach our children about the *Great Wound*, which is Rohr's term for the paschal mystery. Instead, we reduced Christianity to a code of courtesy, which we encourage our children and others to adopt so that the world will be a nicer place. Even worse, we falsely portray Christianity as a blueprint for building a "stone tower of perfection" that we vainly hope will protect us from pain. However, the primary revelation of the paschal mystery, the story of Christ's death and resurrection, is that suffering and pain cannot be avoided or escaped but rather are the very means to a new reality. Any authentic Christian engagement with the third God Question culminates with the paschal mystery becoming the fundamental organizing principle at the core of our being—and the lens through which we understand the meaning of our lives.

Encountering Death

It is evident from reading Marquette's journal that seventeenth-century Christians did not flinch as much from incorporating the mystery of the Great Wound within their understanding of their place in the world and who God was calling them to be. Marquette repeatedly states that he does not fear death, and even alludes that he *welcomes* it, rejoicing in the prospect of dying as a martyr for the faith. Marquette was not alone in living life within the Great Wound. You can hear the nearness of the pascal mystery in his Jesuit superior's account of Marquette death.

Although more needs to be said about Marquette and Jolliet's journey to and down the Mississippi River, let's jump to his final days. Ever since boldly striding into that initial Illinois village, Marquette resolved to return to set up a missionary station and preach the Christian gospel to this tribe. Of course, Marquette and Jolliet first needed to complete their exploration of the Mississippi River and return to the French outposts on the Great Lakes to give their report, which they did in the fall of 1673. Marquette anticipated returning to the Illinois lands as soon as the winter ice cleared from the waterways in the spring of 1674. Sadly, he fell desperately ill that spring and was bedridden that entire summer, only regaining his strength by the fall. Now adequately healthy, he and two companions headed for the Illinois lands, joining a flotilla of Pottawatomie and Illinois traveling in the same direction. They planned to use the "shortcut" path that Marquette and Jolliet learned about during their encounter with the Illinois: canoeing south along the western shore of Lake Michigan, paddling up the Chicago River, portaging over to the Des Plaines River, and then following it to the Illinois villages. Tragically, an early winter often forced the group to camp ashore for days as they waited for the severe winds to abate. Then Marquette's illness returned. By the time they arrived at the Chicago River, it was frozen over.

Marquette was too sick to hike the sixty miles to the Illinois village, so the three men camped in a crude hut for the winter, which further damaged Marquette's health. The next spring, though, Marquette seemed to gain strength as the weather warmed. Hence, they ultimately continued to the Illinois village, arriving on the Wednesday of Holy Week (April 10, 1675). Marquette preached the gospel and celebrated open-air Masses throughout the Triduum. But his health was precipitously deteriorating once again. Thus, after celebrating Easter Sunday Mass, his companions repacked their canoe because Marquette desperately needed medical attention.

As they furiously paddled back upriver and then along the

eastern shore of Lake Michigan, Marquette's health further declined. His companions recounted his final day, which Marquette's Jesuit superior described in a letter back to France:

> The evening before his death, which was a Friday, he told them, very joyously, that it would take place on the morrow....He spoke of all these things with such great tranquility and peace of mind that one might have supposed he was concerned with the death and burial of another person rather than his own. He conversed with them thus as they made their way along the lake until, perceiving a river on whose shores stood an eminence which he deemed well suited as the place of his interment, he told them that that was the place of his last repose....They accordingly brought him to the land, lighted a little fire for him, and prepared for him a wretched bark shelter....

> They drew near him and he embraced them once again, while they burst into tears at his feet. Then he asked them for holy water and his reliquary; and having himself removed his crucifix, which he always carried suspended around his neck, he placed it in the hands of one of his companions, begging him to hold it before his eyes.... Fixing his eyes on the crucifix, he declared in clear, calm tones that he died a Christian, a son of the Holy Roman Catholic Church...and gave thanks to the divine majesty for the great favor accorded him of dying in the Society of Jesus, of dying in it as a missionary of Jesus Christ, and, above all, of dying, as he had always prayed, in a wretched cabin in the midst of the forests and bereft of all human succor....

> He charged his companions to remind him, when they saw he was about to expire, to repeat frequently the names of Jesus and Mary, if he could not do so himself. They did as

they were bidden; and when they believed him to be near his end, one of them called aloud, "Jesus, Mary!" The dying man repeated the words distinctly, several times; and, as if at these sacred names, something appeared to him, suddenly he raised his eyes above his crucifix, holding them riveted on that apparition, which he appeared to regard with pleasure. So, with a countenance beaming and aglow, he peacefully rendered his blessed soul to his creator on Saturday, May 18, between eleven and midnight. (Donnelly, *Marquette*, 258–259)

Two years and one day from the start of his famous expedition to the Mississippi River and fourteen days before the thirty-eighth celebration of his birth into the human adventure on life's river, Marquette completed his ongoing journey to the Immense Waters. His companions buried him in this tranquil view above the river flowing into the dark-blue lake. They planted a large cross at his feet, returned to their canoe, and continued their own journey home.

Marquette's final hours have undoubtedly been embroidered with hagiographic threads. However, the very fact that these appear as discordant seams to our eyes should tell us something about ourselves. Until our modern age, death was cheap—a constant companion. The people of those past centuries lived with the Great Wound. They had no other choice. They *knew* that the third God Question required placing the Great Wound at the center of God's care. Senseless? *Yes.* Paradoxical? *Yes.* True? *Yes.*

Passioning Commitment

While the Great Wound was in the seventeenth-century air, Marquette also was well formed within it through his Jesuit training. The Third Week or Movement of Ignatius' *Spiritual Exercises* is devoted to praying with the Passion of Jesus. Ignatius instructs us to ask for the following grace during the Third Week: "I...pray for the gift of being able to feel sorrow with Jesus in sorrow, to be anguished with Jesus's anguish, and even to experience tears and deep grief because of all the afflictions which Jesus endures for me" (Fleming, *Draw Me Into Your Friendship,* 153). The challenge in this Third Movement of the *Spiritual Exercises* is to experience Jesus' journey to the cross with the same amount of passion, torment, and pathos as we do when someone we know and love deeply is being swept away from us toward the abyss of death. We are to seek to enter into that pain with all the feeling that is possible—to ache for our friend, Jesus.

Death has a way of clarifying our lives. It strips every relationship down to its essence. It tells us who our real friends are, because they are the ones who stay with us, visit us, and console us. After all, a person slipping away on a hospital bed has no "value" in the way the world defines value. They are not people with whom we can go out to a restaurant for entertaining conversation; they are not productive workers in a going enterprise; they are not even people who can walk over to a neighbor's house to give emotional counsel and support. The person who is dying is a person who cannot give, because he or she is busy giving his or her very life to that all-consuming thing called death. Those who sit in vigil at the foot of the bed of a dying person are not the "party" friends, the "work" friends, or the "neighbor" friends. No, all that is left are our true friends, those whose love for us is not based on our "usefulness" to them, but rather their commitment to us.

Thus, death also has a way of sealing our commitments. In an ironic way, death takes us back to our baptisms as infants. At baptism, our parents made a commitment to raise us up in the faith, to bear us into the presence of God through their love. Likewise, as someone approaches death, family and friends once again, by *their* commitment to be present with the dying person, lovingly bear the person in those final hours toward the ultimate entry into God's presence. *Commitment.* That is what death calls us to, challenges us to, draws us to. *Commitment.*

According to Ignatius, one of the sought-for graces of the Third Movement of the *Spiritual Exercises* is a real confirmation of and commitment to those choices that we discern in prayer with the gospel stories. If those decisions are of the Spirit, we seek to forge our wills toward this end. Just as iron is melted in the blast furnace so it might be hammered and shaped into unbending steel, so too this red-hot journey of love with Jesus to his cross should evermore conform our will to this purpose of God. Ironically (no pun intended), though, the only way to develop an iron will is by maintaining an ever-compassionate heart—a heart that aches for the pain of the world. This is the paradox of the cross: it steels our will by keeping our hearts pliable. For this very reason, the cross must be at the heart of our understanding of the third God Question.

Carrying Bones

After a peaceful sleep, Micah and I awake feeling as if we are beginning to bake. The intense, bright sun is already converting our dome tent into a warm oven. This would turn out to be the hottest day on the Russell River Rendezvous. As I make breakfast, Micah explores the island's wide sandy swath. He quickly retraces his steps to show me a rather disquieting discovery. "Dad," he says, "look over at that next island, across the channel. There's a dead whitetail deer lying on the shore." We stare at the lifeless carcass, encased within a cloud of flies, and buzz ourselves about the possible causes of its demise.

I go back to my breakfast duties, and Micah resumes his island exploration. He returns to tell me about a mystifying large circle that a previous party had traced in the sand. "It looks like they pitched their tent in the middle of it," Micah reports. I offer a hypothesis: "Maybe they dug a trench in case the water rose during the night." Shaking his head, Micah dissents, "That wouldn't make sense. It was only a couple inches deep. It would have been pretty useless if that was what they were trying to do." With the puzzle unsolved but breakfast completed, we break camp and pack the canoe.

We paddle away, not realizing that on the river banks there rest molded signs composed with the ground that are much more mysterious than a deer corpse and a sand-scrapped circle. Only later would we learn that the highest concentration of effigy mounds in the world exists in southern Wisconsin, and they are particularly clustered along this lower section of the Wisconsin River. Indeed, one of the most remarkable groupings is located on the north shore just past Muscoda, right across from the island where we slept that night.

What are effigy mounds? A little history of human inhabitation of this area is first in order. Based on the archaeological evidence, humans were first present along the Wisconsin River ten thousand years ago, in 8000 BCE. In the earliest discovered graves, dating from about 1000 BCE, the deceased were covered with red ocher and buried with various items that signified their wealth in cemeteries located on high hills.

A shift occurs with the rise of the stunning Hopewell culture, which was established in this region around the time of Christ. The Hopewell created flourishing trade routes that stretched all the way from the eastern seaboard to the Rocky Mountains, from the Gulf of Mexico to Lake Superior. Around the same time that Jesus was buried in a tomb, these people of the Hopewell period living around the Wisconsin River began a new burial practice. They dug a trench on a bluff or hill that usually overlooked a river, lake, or spring. When a person died, the deceased was laid in the trench next to the last person placed there. The body was usually cremated and then covered with dirt. Instead of being buried with valuable items, symbols of rebirth, renewal, and fertility (white sand, mucky soils, clam shells) were placed with the deceased. Once the trench was filled to capacity, which could take years, dirt was piled high over the spot until a large conical or linear mound was formed. Even today, some of these mounds still stand six feet high.

Some archaeologists believe the conical mounds were de-signed to imitate the shape of the former high-hilled cemeteries, while others (drawing on Native American mythology) contend that the circular shape was meant to confuse evil spirits. Perhaps the linear mounds were meant to represent snakes or the tails of water spirits, which were believed to be the guardians of the underworld.

As often happens in human history, new technologies changed the dynamics and ushered in a new culture, called the Late Woodland era (700–1200 CE). A new innovation, the bow and arrow, replaced the spear, making hunting a much more ef-ficient enterprise. Next, corn as a domesticated crop spread from Mexico, providing the residents in the upper Midwest with a stable and nutritious food source. The combination of these two advances transformed their society from hunter-gatherer bands to corn-farming villagers. Some archaeologists have called this shift "perhaps one of the most revolutionary developments to have occurred in the 12,000-year cultural history of North America" (Birmingham and Esenberg, *Indian Mounds of Wisconsin*, 101). Such massive change dictated finding new ways of expressing their sense of God's care for them, especially for the dead.

New realities always open afresh all the God Questions and inevitably mean that the nature of our relationship to the divine must be reconceptualized. During this Late Woodlands period, the simple, geometrically shaped mounds were transformed into elaborate forms in the shape of birds, bears, water lizards—and even horned humans. These new shapes often were placed next to the old conical and linear mounds and always near water sources. More than 15,000 individual mounds were built during this time, but always in clusters, thus creating more than 900 groupings consisting of various effigy shapes in Wisconsin. Some mound figures were immense, stretching to a length of 700 feet (one-eighth of a mile). One eagle figure among the group on the river's bank near our previous night's campsite had a wingspan that stretched a quarter mile!

The communal coordination required to physically construct these sophisticated shapes indicates the evolution of complex societal structures, as well as a more intricate belief system. The chosen shapes were not accidental but rather represented the manitou spirits that the people believed govern the three realms of the universe: air, land, and water. The Thunderbird or eagle (including horned humanoids) was associated with the Upperworld. Customarily the bear and, less commonly, other animals (buffalo, wolf, deer, and so on) were built to represent the earthly realm. Finally, Horned Water Spirits (abnormally shaped lizards, which sometimes are described as water panthers) represented the world of water in the Lowerworld.

Beguilingly, these new types of mounds were bone reliquaries, not graves. Unlike the older conical mounds, people were not placed here immediately upon death. Rather, only their bones, typically devoid of all flesh, are found in the mounds, usually positioned in the head or heart region of the effigy figure. These new mounds were still common graves, with multiple individuals in each mound, but the bodies were all placed in the mound at the same time and the effigy figure was then immediately built over them. Rocks and stones, arranged to form an altar on which offerings were burned, also are found in the mounds. As with conical mounds, symbolic offerings of colored soils, mucky charcoal, and burnt ash are also present in some mounds. Finally and surprisingly, not all the mounds served as burial sites, as some do not contain bones, although altars and offerings were still normally buried in these bone-absent mounds.

What does all this mean? Archaeologists believe that the Late Woodland people would gather each summer at these sacred sites, with each village bringing the bones of those who had died during the previous year. As part of other religious ceremonies, the bones would be interned, offerings would be made, and the whole community would then work together shoulder-to-shoulder to encase their deceased loved ones within the heart of the earth, shaped in the form of an animal that represented the Spirit World. If there were no bodies to be buried that summer, they still built an effigy mound as part of the seasonal rhythm of their religious life.

Therefore these effigy mound clusters are not really graveyards, but cathedrals. They are worship spaces, sanctified by the bones of their dearly departed. The mounds are ritual places to which the people returned year after year for the purpose of reinforcing and renewing what the anthropologists call a "lifeway," which strove to maintain the balance and harmony in the world. Even the typical location of these earthen mounds—on high bluffs that touch the sky overlooking water, the source of life—indicates an attempt to unify the three spheres of their universe: air, land, and water.

The image of these villagers carrying the bones of their beloved, almost as if on pilgrimage, to these great outdoor cathedrals is striking. What an experience it must be to bear the bones of your parent, spouse, or even a child on your back, and joining their bones to those of other deceased members of the tribe as they are laid within the womb of the earth. And then, with the entire community working beside you, transforming their burial place into a manifestation of the spirit's presence.

Our modern cultural customs do not engage the bereavement process so profoundly, so immediately, or so tenderly. When it happens, it occurs almost accidentally. When ovarian cancer took my mother's life more than fifteen years ago, she donated her body to a university medical school. Nine months later, my father received the urn of her cremated remains. That Easter, we traveled to my hometown to spend the holiday with him. We arrived at my childhood home on Good Friday and Dad heartily greeted us. In the midst of the welcoming conversation, my father pointed to a covered vase on the piano and nonchalantly said, "There's your mom." Feeling uneasy, I indignantly sputtered, "You're leaving it out like a decoration?" My father responded, "As you know, we're interring her ashes on the one-year anniversary of her death. So I had to think of the best place to keep her until then. It didn't seem right to put her on the upstairs closet shelf or in the basement storage room. So I thought it best to keep her here, in the living room. It's kind of comforting, actually, to have her here with me. And besides, she loved that piano. She could never play it worth a lick, but she loved it."

This story raises a profound question: Where do we place our pain? Do we cling to it by refusing to allow our wounds to be healed? Hide it overhead by simplistically claiming that our reward for our sufferings will come in heaven? Submerge it underfoot by repressing our memories? How do we travel in life with *our* urn of ash-white hurts, deceased dreams, and lifeless failures? How do we place our disappointments, betrayals, sufferings, and, yes, even death itself, into our sense of the meaning of life?

These are simply different versions of the third God Question. They are not easy questions during the best of times, but they become even more difficult in tumultuous eras like ours. Like the period of the Late Woodland people, our society is rapidly changing. We have not even begun to recognize the massive psychological, social, cultural, and spiritual impact of our modern technologies: computers, cell phones, Internet, and the like. Recent events in the world have exacerbated our sense of being a people in a state of drift. Some of the dependable moorings of life—the stability of the world order; the strength of our economy; the confidence in our religious, political, and business leaders—seem to have become less secure. Furthermore, the very pace of normal life seems to be evermore turbulent with each passing year as we are tossed about by waves of swelling demands and cresting expectations on our jobs, with our families, and from our society. Our feeling of being bound to a safe place in the sea of life, that is, our sense of who we are and what we are called to be, subsequently has become loosened to some degree.

In such a time, our search for locating God's care and presence in our lives becomes heightened, sharpened, and maybe even more imperative. In these moments of distress, we often turn with a new intensity to our faith in hopes of perceiving through the murky, chaotic waters of everyday life the bedrock of existence so that we might lash ourselves to the unmovable rock of ultimate meaning. In fact, the very word *religion* comes from a Latin word that means "to bind together." We want our lives tightly knotted with meaning, with purpose.

In these disorienting times, though, the necessary response is to dive more deeply and freely into the waters of our faith so we can learn again how to carry bones. The lesson of the cross is this: place them next to us—between us and our friend Jesus. The journey with our friend Jesus to his cross must start with us recognizing that Jesus takes up our sin, pain, and suffering on the cross so that they might be redeemed within his sacrificial love.

In other words, the great challenge of the third God Question in the twenty-first century is to learn how to place *our* pain within *the* pain. Henri Nouwen eloquently expressed it this manner:

> The situation which brought about your pain was simply the form in which you came in touch with the human condition of suffering. Your pain is the concrete way in which you participate in the pain of humanity. Paradoxically, therefore, healing means moving from *your* pain to *the* pain. When you keep focusing on the specific circumstances of your pain, you easily become angry, resentful, and even vindictive. You are inclined to do something about the externals of your pain in order to relieve it; this explains why you often seek revenge. But real healing comes from realizing that your own particular pain is a share in humanity's pain. That realization allows you to forgive your enemies and enter into a truly compassionate life. That is the way of Jesus, who prayed on the cross: "Father forgive them; they do not know what they are doing" (Luke 23:34). Jesus' suffering, concrete as it was, was the suffering of all humanity. *His* pain was *the* pain. (Nouwen, *The Inner Voice of Love*, 103–104)

This is where the third God Question takes us: to the cross so that through it we can enter into the Mystery.

Shifting Sands

As we canoe down the river, Micah and I enjoy the great weather. Sunny and hot. Of all of our four sons, Micah's skin is the most sensitive. He slathers on the sunblock, but to little avail, as he will end the day with a nasty burn. By midmorning, we anchor the boat in shallow water in the middle of the river—supposedly to try our luck fishing along a precipitous dropoff, but also to enjoy the river's cooling presence.

We walk to the edge of the dropoff's rim. The river's current tugs at our legs as we cast into this deep pool, which has all the markings of holding big fish. We work along the edge of the dropoff not only because this increases our chances of stumbling across a fish, but also because our feet slowly sink into the sand if we stand in one place too long. Surely some sort of physics is involved with the water's current, the weight of our bodies, and the soft sand, but our feet feel as if they are being magnetically dragged deeper and deeper into the riverbed. If we stand too long in one place, it takes great effort to pull our feet from their sandy twelve-inch graves, and we invariably flounder and flail as we try to keep our balance in the water. We quickly learn that it is best *not* to reel in our lines before attempting such extractions; a swinging treble-hooked lure swaying all about one's pitching body greatly increases the apprehension of the moment.

Actually, this entire riverbed is constantly on the move. Because this lower portion of the Wisconsin descends at a gentle eighteen-inch-per-mile rate, the water is neither cutting down nor building up the riverbed. Rather, the river erodes the soil horizontally, scooping sediment from the outside of a bend and depositing it on the inside of the next bend.

This process has three results. First, the sandbars are constantly migrating downstream. Most move quite slowly, but some travel more than an eighth of a mile over a year. So the river literally carries its riverbed with it, as evidenced by the fact that ten tons of sediment passes by Muscoda *every single day.* Second, the shoreline is constantly changing. This forces the few small towns along the Wisconsin to be set well back from the river, out of both visual range and earshot. This precaution was learned the hard way. A once-prosperous nineteenth-century settlement of a thousand residents, Richland City, was literally eroded completely away in a quick span of thirty-five years when the river began to eat into the town's bank. Various engineering fixes were undertaken, but all to no avail. Thus towns like Muscoda, whose city limits buttress right up to the river's edge, are the exception. Third, the river's ever-shifting and channel-twisting character renders it innavigable for larger boats. It is even rare to see smaller motorized boats because misjudgment in the direction of the meandering channel makes it easy to direct a boat into shallow waters with their propeller-damaging stumps and pin-shearing rocks. And so these idiosyncratic traits allow the river to retain its wilderness feeling, a characteristic that state law and public ownership of the shoreline now maintain into perpetuity.

Both Micah and I have big strikes, but we are unable to set the hook on the unseen watery brutes. Maybe it is for the best, as Marquette reports that his band came across some rather disturbing fish:

> On another occasion, we saw on the water a monster with a head of a tiger, a sharp nose like that of a skunk, with whiskers and straight, erect ears; the head was gray and the neck quite black. We saw no more creatures of this sort. When we cast our nets into the water, we caught sturgeons, and a very extraordinary kind of fish. It resembles the trout, but its mouth is larger and near its nose—which is smaller, as are its eyes; it is a large thing,

shaped like a woman's bust, three fingers wide and a
cubit long, at the end of which is a disk as wide as one's
hand. (*JR*, 195)

With fish like this in the Mississippi river ways, no wonder the
Late Woodland people depicted the water spirit as some sort of
weird horned panther-lizard!

Even though we don't catch any fish, we are refreshed. We
continue our canoeing. This section of the river is quite beautiful,
as the dramatic river bluffs crowd close to the river. We have not
bumped into many people on any of the legs of the journey and
thus this section of the river is particularly quiet. The entire left
bank along this stretch has been designated as a wildlife refuge.
In its midst is the Blue River Barrens, which has active sand dunes
and its own unique ecosystem that supports animals and plant
life, such as cactus, which are typically found in southern desert
regions; this is truly a region out of place.

After making good progress, we decide to stop for lunch.
We see a pair of islands that almost look like twins in the water.
We choose the one on the left and beach the canoe. We lug the
lunch bag and the collapsible folding chairs ashore. I think I
have been quite resourceful in bringing one of those jars of jelly
intermingled with peanut butter, but Micah has other opinions.
"Dad, what is this? Too lazy to open *two* jars and wash *two*
knives?" I laugh at Micah's joke. He continues, "Who do you
think thought up this peanut-butter-and-jelly-in-one-jar idea,
anyway? It must have been some guy who eats over the sink." I
laugh harder, for Micah is now clearly zeroing in on my quirks.
After a recent trip to visit my father, he noticed that I have the
same habit as my father: we both eat sandwiches or other quick
lunches over the sink so that we don't mess up a plate. I find the
practice quite efficient and totally reasonable; Micah describes it
as comical. Clearly enjoying this line of repartee, Micah adopts a
concerned look when I hand a sandwich to him and he exclaims,
"Dad, how are you going to eat? There's not a sink around here!"

We continue trading good-natured barbs, chuckling as we eat our sandwiches, carrots, and apples.

After finishing our lunch, we stretch out on the sand and enjoy a little siesta. Our inactivity encourages the return of the waterfowl that we scared away on our arrival. The water between our island and the southern bank is quite shallow; it is more marsh than river. First, the little sandpipers dart randomly and comically in the shallow water. Next, ducks emerge and begin paddling among the reeds. Then a magnificent blue heron arrives and strides gracefully and majestically through the water. Next, a bald eagle, the first of many that we would see that day, rides the air currents in slow circles. Such life appears when one is quiet!

Wombful Compassion

I look over at Micah as he rests. It is always easy to be in his presence. He is patient and comfortable with waiting for the right moment to move on. He has a certain intentionality about him. He is diligent in completing tasks, but he doesn't rush absently through life. He is sensitive and kindhearted. A gentle, generous person.

From his time in the womb, he has been like this. My wife says that, among all our sons, he was the most tranquil during pregnancy. And he certainly did not hurry to come out, as he was finally induced two weeks past the due date. He emerged weighing ten pounds and two ounces—quite a size considering that my wife is only five feet tall. He was definitely wombful!

Wombful. That fits Micah quite well, if we understand the term as it was used in Jesus' day. Although the gospels are written in Greek, Jesus spoke Aramaic, a Semitic language related to Hebrew, which was the common tongue for those living in Galilee. This means that the word Jesus and his contemporaries used for *womb* was *rehem*. Interestingly, the plural form of womb (*rahamim*) means *compassion* in both Aramaic and Hebrew.

This etymology makes eminent sense. If you are trying to describe the human experience of a person feeling deeply for the suffering, pain, and vulnerability of another person, what is better than using a mother's sense of care and concern for one of her offspring? Does not a mother's biological connection with her child—by the very fact that this person once filled her womb and lived within her—give her a more intimate and uniquely visceral sense of empathetic oneness with that child? If so, then the mother's sympathy for her child embodies the experience that we, in English, strive to capture in the word *compassion*, which derives from Latin and literally means "to suffer with."

There are other reasons to use *wombs* to express the emotion of compassion. The ancients believed that this emotion sprang from the womb (for women) or the guts (for men). Even today, we say "I felt it in my guts" when we have a very traumatic or painful experience. In fact, one of the Greek verbs for compassion is *splanchnizomai*, which is a form of their word for "guts."

That's where I felt my pain during that frightful storm five years ago. While my fear seemed to come from my head, my ache for Micah, my beloved son, was in my guts. I remember looking at his angelic face as he slept, almost weeping because I loved him so much. I wanted his happiness so desperately. This feeling overwhelms me whenever I intentionally slow down and really meditate on those whom I love. It starts in the guts but moves to the heart. The joy is so complete that it…hurts. And yet, that's not the right word. Rather, it…burns. It burns with a passion so deep that it consumes and purges my own petty wants and demands, and I am filled with love.

The absolutely amazing thing is that God loves us in the same way. Jesus gave the following command during his ministry: "Be compassionate as God is compassionate" (see Luke 6:36). Given that Jesus spoke Aramaic, a more literal translation might be: "Be wombful as God is wombful." This directive not only calls us to act with compassion, but also to believe in a God who is "womblike"—a God who feels as deeply for each one of us as a mother feels for her child. For this reason, the Book of Isaiah proclaims, "For thus says the Lord: I will extend prosperity [or peace] to her like a river, and the wealth [or glory] of the nations like an overflowing stream; and you shall nurse and be carried on her arm, and dangled upon her knees. As a mother comforts her child, so I will comfort you" (66:12–13a). *That* is how God cares for us: like a nursing mother who tenderly bears us on her hip and playfully bounces us on her knees. What a loving God!

The third God Question, therefore, must lead us to see God as a comforting mother. We have a God who loves us so much that God responded with *womb-ful love*. God entered a womb to become human so as to share in his children's pains and joys, even though that also meant God must experience the greatest human suffering, death. However, by this love, which continually draws God to us and us to God, darkness is overcome and death is conquered. God did this because...well, just because that's what you do when you're womb-ful.

Quite possibly it was in an effort to lead us to a proper comprehension of the third God Question that Jesus doesn't call God by other perfectly acceptable titles such as "Lord," "Almighty," or "God of Hosts." Instead, Jesus prefers a rather striking, and even bold, name for God: "Father." Unfortunately, using parental language to refer to God does not often stir any mystery in our souls today. After all, we mumble quickly through the Lord's Prayer without a second thought to the power implicit within the first two words: "Our Father."

In contrast, examples abound from New Testament texts that the earliest Christians recognized the profound implications of this parental language. We can almost hear the sense of amazement when the writer of the First Letter of John exclaims, "See what love the Father has given us, that we should be called children of God; and that is what we are....Beloved, we are God's children now" (3:1a–2a). The new revelation that God made known to us through Jesus' birth, life, death, and resurrection is that our relationship with God is so intimate that the only way to capture it is by knowing that we are God's own children. In other words, we come from the very womb of God.

If we take this children of God language seriously, if we not just imagine this as an intriguing figure of speech, but truly believe it, then it not only changes our sense of place and calling in the world, but also our appreciation of our own families. Suddenly, our roles in our families become powerful experiences of God's presence. For example, parents' bottomless love for their children teaches a deep insight about the human person's relationship with God: life is not a test with the goal of earning God's love by being good; rather life is fundamentally an experience of God's love that calls forth goodness from us in response. Love between spouses reflects the divine love of the three persons in the Trinity for each other. Our love for our parents mirrors Jesus' fidelity to his Father. Further, our love for our fellow brothers and sisters reflects our Christian commitment to love one another. Our challenge, therefore, is for our families to bear the awesome mystery of God's love by our love.

Yet, it goes beyond even our families. If we really become wombful people, then we feel the entire world's pain and need. This is why Ignatius spends so much time in the *Spiritual Exercises* encouraging us to pray with the cross, because it is the way to becoming fully compassionate. Often we feel so powerless in the face of the immensity of social ills and dire needs that we excuse ourselves from engaging them. Our rationalization becomes "I can't solve the problem, so why even try?" However, the experience of Christ's cross requires more of us. As David Fleming notes:

> In a similar way, we experience a question rising within us about staying with Jesus at this time of his passion. His passion is history; we can do nothing to change it. We want to escape from a painful situation where we seemingly can do nothing. Ignatius strongly emphasizes how we must "labor" in our praying in this Week. Compassion is hard because it results only in our involved presence, when relieving action on our part is impossible

or negligible. As we allow Jesus to help us enter into his passion, we find that the grace of compassion leads to a new depth of relationship with Jesus. We experience that the love of compassion must be an integral part of the love of service *(Like the Lightning, 25)*.

Certainly love involves tragedy because love can only exist if we risk feeling one another's pain and the mess of the world. In the end, though, God's wombful love for us is an embodied reality, embodied in enduring, complicated, and fragile relationships of love, that draws us to remain with the world's pain, even when we cannot solve that pain. Praying with the cross invariably reminds us that fidelity to our call means responding with love, serving with love, remaining with love.

So the third God Question directs us to a rather profound insight: the way God cares for us is the manner in which we are to care for each other and the world—with compassion. While each of us might have a particular vocation, this call is universal. We are all to be wombful as our Father is wombful.

Dead Ends

After our siesta, Micah and I pack up our lunch supplies and continue down the river. Because the Wisconsin is continually shifting in its banks, it sometimes cuts a radically new channel. As sediment builds up between the river's new course and the old way, the former channel becomes a separate shallow lake or swamp, called a slough. In some cases, the disengagement is only partial, as some of these sloughs remain connected to the main river via a creek. These transformed backwaters are often brimming with waterfowl and other aquatic wildlife.

Our map notes that we will pass a slough that has one creek entering it upstream and another exiting it downstream. We decide to explore it since we will not need to backtrack to return to the river. We quickly discover that this slough is indeed shallow. Many times we have to get out of the canoe and walk it to deeper water. It is the middle of the afternoon, which means two things. One, it is really hot. Two, since it is hot, the wildlife is not zipping around the slough, but hanging in the shade. Disappointing. Our progress is slow and sweaty. Maybe following this abandoned river channel is a mistake.

The old ways are indeed not always the best ways. For example, while Marquette's journal records many positive comments about various Indian tribes, it also reveals a certain European hubris in his encounters with the native peoples. His zeal in spreading the gospel stems from an obviously deep love of Christ, but it sometimes blinds him to the religious integrity and cultural achievements within the Native American cultures. For example, he is mystified by a cliff painting the expedition observes on the Mississippi because he doubts that the native people could have accomplished such a fine piece of artwork.

> While skirting some frightfully huge rocks, we saw upon one of them two monsters painted there that startled us at first. Even the boldest Indians dare not rest their eyes on them for long. They are large as a calf, with horns on their heads like those of a deer, a horrible look, red eyes, a beard like a tiger's, a face somewhat like a man's, a body covered with scales, and a long tail that encircles the body, passing above the head and going back between the legs, ending in a fish's tail. Green, red, and black are the three colors composing the picture. These two monsters were so well painted that we could not believe that they were executed by a savage. The best artists of France could not have done better, especially if they had to paint on such high and inaccessible rocks. (*JR*, 205)

Marquette was not alone in his biases. When Europeans stumbled on the effigy mounds, they too doubted that "savages" could produce such awe-inspiring earthen sculptures. Their prejudices forced them to concoct wild theories. Some believed that Europeans had landed in America in the distant past and had built them. Certainly Vikings arrived along the shores of North America before Columbus ran into Hispaniola in 1492, but they never ventured inland. Another popular hypothesis is that the Ten Lost Tribes of Israel had migrated to America. This speculation was fueled by the recognition that the mythological stories of the native peoples had certain resonances with Judeo-Christian tenets of faith. Joseph Smith, of course, incorporated a version of this assumption into the Mormon faith. Even today some contend that such architectural artifacts are the works of aliens who arrived by spaceship.

The grandeur and greatness of many pre-Columbian civilizations in the Americas are only now becoming clear. At the same time, our understanding of the devastating effect of European contact on these civilizations is also becoming evident, and it is a story of holocaust. New studies estimate that more people lived in the Americas than in Europe in 1491, but that within the first 130 years after Columbus' arrival as many as 95 percent of the people living in America died due to European disease. That means that a stunning 80 to 100 million people—between 600,000 and 750,000 per year—died by the date of Marquette's birth. As Charles C. Mann points out in his book *1491*, European viruses spread to native populations well in advance of face-to-face encounters. Such decimation had traumatic effects on the level of cultural sophistication of the survivors. Some developed immunities and population numbers stabilized, but the advance of European diseases, in a very real way, bombed the more complex tribal societies back to the Stone Ages.

What a travesty! What an indictment! How callous those Europeans settlers were. While the effects might have been unintentional, don't they deserve our scorn for their blindness to the devastation that they wrought on these innocent people? Should we not heap condemnation on them for privileging their own needs, for the expansion of trade, and for the conversion of souls to their way of life, above the physical survival of these people? Yes. Definitely yes!

But then, our denunciation of them surely renders us even more culpable for the modern-day mass murder that results from our own lifestyle. Every year, roughly eight million people die worldwide due to hunger; six million are children younger than five years of age. Of that number, only 5 to 10 percent is the result of famine caused by drought or disaster due to social disruptions such as war. The vast majority die because the world's food resources are not equitably distributed. Simple math demonstrates that the world produces enough food to feed everyone. So eight million people die each year because we don't share the food we have with them.

Eight million people a year! That is *ten times* as many people who died each year during the American holocaust caused by European diseases. Shouldn't the number of dead shock us out of our complacency? After all, that means 22,000 people, more than 16,000 of whom are innocent children, are dying every single day because I am eating more than I need to survive and because I am part of a culture that does not have the necessary compassion to change the system by which we distribute food to those in need. Why don't we care enough? Is it because the number is so big that it seems that we are talking about statistics and not actual people? If you read at the average speed for an adult, then ten people died of hunger while you were reading this one paragraph. Ten! Fifteen a minute, one every four seconds. Count to four. One. Two. Three. Four. A person just died due to the deficiency of our care, the weakness of our will, the insufficiency of our compassion.

You might respond that you are not to blame because you give to a hunger charity or you are a vegetarian and therefore eat lower on the food chain. These are good and holy actions. However, they do not absolve us from our common guilt. It has been estimated that world hunger can be eradicated for the cost of $13 billion a year. That sounds like a large number, but it is actually a pittance. It is the equivalent of each citizen in the United States donating a measly $50 each year. It is even more infinitesimal if put into budgetary terms. The U.S. federal budget is $2.8 *trillion.* So if only 0.05% of the entire U.S. budget was dedicated to this goal each year, we could end world hunger. That is one-half of a hundredth of a percent. And we solve it!

But we as a nation, which certainly has the financial resources to easily conquer this problem, simply stand by as...one, two, three, four...people die and die and die and die. We are all culpable; no one is exempt. We are all part of the problem because we could very easily be part of the solution. It's our social sin, and we cannot extract ourselves from it by blaming weak politicians or market forces. If we had the compassion, this would change. As a people, we plainly do not care enough. We value $50 more than eight million people.

So any honest engagement of the third God Question inherently makes us aware of a humble truth: we don't care enough. Admitting that fact is essential in living an authentic life of faith, for it points to the reality of what is traditionally called original sin: our human nature is such that we just don't care enough. Only God cares enough. We, on the other hand, always live in the limitations of our care, our compassion, our love. Thus, only God's love can heal and make whole our incompleteness.

If we really, honestly ask the third God Question, we are startled by a sorrowful realization: my present-day sins stab Jesus' heart just as surely as the Roman-day nails pierced his flesh. Jesus' crucifixion is not a one-time event but an ongoing actuality. The cross is not just something that Jesus is pinned to but a reality that we enter into by directly meeting our own pain in the crucifixion of Christ.

Oh, how we hate to hear that message! A priest friend of mine once shared with me a nasty letter that he had received from a parishioner. The letter was critical, blunt, and unsigned. However, the object of this parishioner's anger was not some moral position the priest had taken in a homily, nor some policy adopted by the parish council...nor even about money! Rather, this anonymous, faceless parishioner complained that he didn't like the dramatic reading of the passion on Palm Sunday because he thought it unfair and inappropriate for the congregation to take the role of the crowd by shouting, "*Crucify him! Crucify him!*"

Lifting our voices to shout "*Crucify, crucify!*" *is* a disturbing thing, and it *should* make our skin crawl. That is why we do it: to remind ourselves that we are part of the passion story. The rejection and killing of Jesus was not just something that *those* people did, back *then,* and over *there.* It was not the fault of the Jews, or the religious authorities, or the Romans, or any other *faceless* "them." The rejection and killing of Jesus is a reality of sin in which we, too, are involved. When we hate to hear our own voices say "*Crucify, crucify!*" then we are brought face-to-face with our own complicity in sin, the part that we play in rejecting Jesus even here and now.

In many ways, we are not so different. Like the crowd in front of Pilate, we find it too easy to accept violence in our society as an everyday thing. How often do we shrug off the gruesome bloodshed on the world stage, the vitriolic tone within our national debates, the brutalizing social conditions in our cities, and even our own angry words toward our loved ones as just "the way things are" in life? When we do, we, too, are part of the story about a crowd that crucifies Christ.

Like the crowd in front of Pilate, we too often slip into a mob mentality in which we allow our values to be compromised by our desire for the respect and acceptance by others. How often do we find our devotion to Jesus ebbing and flowing with the cultural currents that swirl around us? When we do, we, too, are part of the story about a crowd that crucifies Christ.

Like the crowd in front of Pilate, we live in a political system that often seems to favor the rich and the powerful at the expense of the weak and vulnerable. How often do we turn our backs on the poor and those on the fringes who would have an equal share of our power? When we do, we, too, are part of the story about a crowd that crucifies Christ.

But there is more to the story than our coming face-to-face with our own complicity in sin. There is more to the story because after we read the passion, we celebrate the Eucharist; after the story of Jesus' death, we share the bread and cup that is the promise of Christ's life. After we hear with horror how our voices shout "*Crucify!*" we raise our voices again to say, "Lamb of God, who takes away the sins of the world, have mercy upon us" and "Christ has died, Christ has risen, Christ will come again." There is more to the story because the story of Jesus points beyond sin to the promise of forgiveness, beyond hate to the triumph of love, beyond crucifixion to the good news of the resurrection.

Ultimately, the third God Question is about good news. We come face-to-face with our sin in the passion, but only so that Christ may bring us face-to-face with forgiveness. We hate to say "*Crucify!*" but only so that we may learn how much we love to say "*Hosanna!*" We play the part of rejecting Jesus, but only so that we feel more deeply the reality of accepting Jesus. This good news is the triumph of love told in the story of the passion that resides at the center of the third God Question...and this is the love that blesses us today.

Confirming Forgiveness

Hot and tired, Micah and I finally emerge from the slough. We beach the canoe and gratefully dive into the cool water, enjoying a refreshing swim. We toss a football and find that it is imperative to catch the ball or else the current, which is quite strong, quickly washes it downstream. Observing this, I happen upon an idea. "Hey, Micah, let's put on lifejackets and race." Micah looks at me disdainfully. "Dad, I don't think I need to wear a lifejacket. I'm not a little kid. I can swim." I smile and then explain, "Here's how this race will work. We put on the lifejackets and float down the river. We can't kick or do any swim strokes. All we can do is float. The first one to make it to the other end of the island wins."

So we don our lifejackets and begin our slow-motion race. We quickly learn that there is more to this floating business than one might initially assume. First, we discover that it is best to start the race in the deeper water or else our bodies bump along the river bottom. Not a pleasant experience. Second, the skill of floating efficiently is rather difficult. The temptation to paddle is strong, especially since a slight lean easily leads to a face full of water. The key seems to be to just let go—to surrender to the current so that it cradles and carries us.

Maybe such an experience led Denise Levertov, in her poem "The Avowal," to pen these words:

> *As swimmers dare*
> *to lie face to the sky*
> *and water bears them,*
> *as hawks rest upon air*
> *and air sustains them,*
> *so would I learn to attain*
> *freefall, and float*
> *into Creator Spirit's deep embrace,*
> *knowing no effort earns*
> *that all-surrounding grace.*

Grace. Indeed it is saving. Sin is intractable and insidious, but grace is redemptive. We are born and borne within grace.

Our Christian belief is that sin does not have the last word because it is not as powerful as God's grace. Grace is the power of God to overcome the effects of sins to restore us to live in God's love (see Ephesians 2:4–10; Titus 3:4–7). Karl Rahner, the foremost Catholic theologian of the twentieth century, described grace as God's self-communication—the sharing of God's divinity with us. The Eastern Christian tradition talked about grace as "divinization"—the partaking in the life of God. Hence, we might say that grace is an unmerited gift imprinted on humanity's being by which we participate in the being and life of God. Startlingly, Jesus taught that the means to this "divinization" was forgiveness—God's forgiveness of our sins and our forgiveness of each other's trespasses.

After half a dozen grace-races, Micah and I finally clamber out of the water, dry off, and cast our canoe back into the water. As we paddle, we begin to discuss Micah's upcoming junior year in high school. He will run cross-country in the fall and is looking forward to trying out for the school musical. In our archdiocese, the sacrament of confirmation is received during junior year, so Micah will start participating in the preparation classes.

I ask, "Have you thought about the saint's name you'll take as your confirmation name?" Micah responds, "No. Not really." We are silent for awhile. Then, an idea hits me. "Micah, I've got it. The perfect name!" "What?" he inquires cautiously. "Well, Mom and I named you 'Micah' because the first reading at our wedding was from the prophet Micah—the reading about how God wants three things from us: to act justly, love tenderly, and walk humbly with our God. And your middle name, John, came from the second reading that we picked for our wedding, which was about how God is love and whoever lives in love, lives in God, and God lives in them." Leerily, Micah answers with a slow "Yes." In contrast, I am getting excited. "Well, why don't you pick 'Matthew' for your confirmation name because the gospel reading of our wedding came from that gospel. It was from Jesus' Sermon on the Mount when he told people not to worry about making ends meet. That God provides food for the birds of the air and clothes the lilies. What counts are the things of God's kingdom—righteousness, forgiveness, love. So wouldn't it be cool to choose Matthew so that your name will be Micah John Matthew Russell. Pretty neat, huh?"

Micah looks back at me. I could be wrong, but I think he rolled his eyes. Then he answers, "Well, I was thinking about Paul. You know, after Papa. Paul was Papa's confirmation name." "Oh," I answer, "that would be good, too. That is, if you want to take the name of a guy who eats over a sink." Micah laughs, but I know that I have put him in an awkward position of choosing between his grandfather's name and my desires. So I shift the focus of the conversation. "So what are you looking forward to the most in connection to confirmation?" Micah shrugs, and then says, "I don't know. I've heard the retreat is supposed to be good."

Micah's instincts are good. Retreats are often blessed times in our journey of faith. They provide us the space to become aware of God's loving, forgiving hand. By breaking our normal routine, we encounter the third God Question in astonishing ways. I once worked with a priest who told me a story from his life that dramatized just such a moment.

It was a confirmation retreat, and there was a crusty core of high-school students who, at their best, oozed with smirking indifference; at their worst, they projected a belligerent resistance. When it was time for the sacrament of reconciliation, the main troublemaker entered the room set up for confessions. He had refused the entire retreat to take off his medal-laden letter jacket to make it inescapably clear that, by being ready to leave at a moment's notice, he wanted to be anywhere but here. Eyes shielded by the bill of his pulled-down baseball cap, he slumped into the chair opposite the priest and said, "That lady in charge said I had to come in here. I don't know why I am here. I don't have any sins to tell. I'm not going to make a confession."

The priest looked intently at the young man for a moment, leaned forward, and said, "Thank God. Because *I* really need to make *my* confession." The priest then took off his stole and placed in on the young man's shoulders. The young man balked but the priest insisted, saying, "No, I really need to confess my sins. Sitting here and hearing all these teenagers share their struggles has made me so aware of the many ways that I have failed to love well. I need to get this stuff off my chest." Then the priest began to recount his sins—all the patterns in his life that harmed himself and others, all his attitudes that prevented him from loving God as God loves him. As the priest shared his vulnerabilities and shortcomings, the young man at first was shocked but soon he became uncomfortable in the presence of this man's open honesty.

Then the priest said, "Now I need you to put your hands on my head and pray the words of absolution." The young man recoiled and said, "I can't." The priest was adamant, "I need to feel God's forgiveness...I need to be reminded that God loves me." The young man extended shaking, hesitant hands. And then, the miracle happened. This rock-hard jock began to cry. He collapsed onto the shoulder of the priest, sobbing as if the dam of his stony heart had suddenly broken open. The same words kept rushing out of the boy, "I'm sorry. I'm sorry. I'm sorry." Slowly, the boy regained composure. He got up and left.

After the retreat ended, the retreat director called the priest to thank him for hearing confessions. Then she said, "I don't know what you said to that ringleader in confession, but he was like a new person in the retreat from then on. He stopped giving me lip and started to participate in the discussions. Once his attitude changed, the rest of them followed. So thanks." The priest chuckled and said, "You know, that retreat director probably thought I read this young man the riot act. If only she knew that all I did was reveal my own brokenness to the boy. Ah, the power of weakness!"

Usually we think of sin as a barrier that blocks us from loving God, and it *is* that. However, it can also be a source of grace because God continues working to redeem us even through our sins. Mark Link makes this point when he wrote: "Our sense of sin is linked to our sense of God. The closer we are to God, the more aware we are of our sinfulness....This is because our distance from God reduces the contrast necessary for us to recognize our true condition" (Link, *Challenge* [1988], 91). His point is not that we should wallow in our sinfulness but to see that absolutely nothing is off-limits to God's love and power. Even sin can be transformed into a portal of grace if we allow God to reorient ourselves to our true selves, which is to say, to orient ourselves toward God's love. God's grace is always drawing us through our weaknesses, not in spite of them.

Praying Generosity

The hot day of paddling ends at the town of Boscobel. The canoe landing is located in an inlet, so Micah and I shoot past the inlet and then paddle mightily against the current to enter this murky back channel. We unload the canoe and load the car. With weary muscles, sunburned skin, and joyous hearts, we head back home.

The Way of the Cross is unavoidable in our lives, but our God not only goes with us, but before us. It is only because of Christ's suffering, death, and resurrection that the Prayer of Generosity, attributed to Saint Ignatius, makes any sense to utter—words Marquette might well have prayed in his moments of toil and terror.

> *Eternal Word, only begotten Son of God,*
> *Teach me true generosity.*
> *Teach me to serve you as you deserve.*
> *To give without counting the cost,*
> *To fight heedless of wounds,*
> *To labor without seeking rest,*
> *To sacrifice myself without thought of any reward*
> *Save the knowledge that I have done your will.*
> *Amen.* (Harter, ed., *Hearts on Fire*, 35)

However, we are not to wallow in our struggle and suffering, but rather be transformed by it. God cares for us with a faithful, motherly love during both times of horror and in moments of humor. God is in it all, because God uses all things to redeem us—to love us. Our task is to live within that truth so that we might become that truth. Or, as an old adage, often quoted by Richard Rohr, expresses it, "The young man who cannot cry is a savage; the old man who cannot laugh is a fool." My prayer is that Micah, and all my sons, become men of tears and delight. For then they will be wombful men.

CHAPTER FOUR

Where Is God's Love?

What is our place in the world?
Who is God calling us to be?
How is God caring for us?
Where is God's love?

Crossing Into Grace

We begin at the end. Standing on a 500-foot-high cliff at the confluence of the Wisconsin and Mississippi rivers, the lush landscape dramatically frames the "T" created by these two rivers' convergence. The dark-green bluffs accentuate the sand-brown color of the rivers. Saturated in panoramic beauty, the merging rivers are transformed into a massive "Tau" cross. I soak in what we will pass through to our ultimate end.

Then, words startle me from my meditation. "Hey, Dad, look at this." I turn to see Ryan, our twenty-year-old second son, crouching in front of a large granite plaque, encased in a stone wall and etched with these words:

At The Foot Of
This Eminence
JACQUES MARQUETTE
and
LOUIS JOLIET
Entered The
Mississippi River
June 17, 1673

Ryan and I are about to begin the fourth and final leg of the Russell River Rendezvous on the Wisconsin River, from Boscobel to the Mississippi. We will park our car at the takeout spot, a county park along the banks of the Mississippi, and the shuttle service will transport us and our gear to the Boscobel put-in location. Ryan and I take advantage of these arrangements to make a short side trip to this magnificent overlook located in Wyalusing State Park.

Before making this detour, I wrestled over whether we should come here at the start of the final stretch of the canoe trip. Somehow it felt like cheating. I had traveled more than seventy-five miles with my other three sons on the river's own level toward this goal—this spot where the Wisconsin merges with the Mississippi. So was it right to preempt the journey by taking in this sight now? Might this spectacular preview subtract from the excitement of entering the Mississippi in our little canoe?

Now, though, I am glad that we have come. From this majestic frame of reference, I can see the awe-inspiring divine tapestry into which we will be weaved as we pass this way. We will not—*are* not—just independent individuals floating through space and time, but rather part of something larger. Our present will be—*is*—connected to something far grander than even this marvelous natural landscape. For we are the creations of a loving Triune God.

Just as Ryan and I needed to see the big picture to contextualize the significance of our forthcoming journey, any engagement with the fourth God Question—*Where is God's love?*—must begin with a view toward the ultimate end: our Triune God. What an audacious claim we Christians make when we profess belief in the Trinity. What, the world might ask, does it mean to say that the one and only God is three persons, Father, Son, and Holy Spirit? From the world's perspective, this is even worse than the philosophically untenable belief in Christ's crucifixion because the Trinity is mathematically impossible. One plus one plus one does not equal one. And one is not the same as three! As one of the early Church Fathers admitted, "When we talk about the Trinity, we must forget how to count."

The Trinity may be bad math, but it is excellent theology. Our doctrine of the Trinity says that at God's essence—at God's deepest core—God exists in relationship. The decisive point of the Trinity is that we believe that God's nature is fundamentally communitarian. God only exists—and can only exist—in community, in a relationship of love.

With this discussion on the Trinity, we step on some slippery sand. The early church struggled ardently, all the way up to the Council of Nicaea in 325 CE, to find adequate terminology—one essence, three persons—to express this mystery. But even this articulation of the doctrine is not crystal clear. Almost a hundred years later, even the formidable mental abilities of Saint Augustine grappled in a lengthy treatise entitled *De Trinitate* (*The Trinity)* to explain the Nicene formulation. He offered this analogy for understanding the Trinity: Since God is Love, then love requires a Lover (God the Father, who initiates the loving), a Beloved (God the Son, who is the object of love), and the act of Loving (God the Holy Spirit, who is the loving energy between Lover and Beloved). But after writing this explanation, Augustine slumped back in his chair and admitted that this analogy is still not sufficiently nuanced to fully capture the Trinitarian relationship. You can almost hear Augustine's exhaustion as he says, in effect, "OK, so, the Trinity is...uhm, well...well, it's all about the effusiveness of God's overflowing love—and who can define how love works exactly? So if love is a mystery, then how much more so is the Trinity! Hence the Trinity is…it's about how God is a relationship of love." By its inherent perplexity, the belief in the Trinity keeps us on the river, for its meaning can only be found in the depths of the questions it raises about the essential nature of All Being, not in the firmness of its answers.

Still, our belief that the core of the Divine Being consists of a loving relationship has big implications for anyone seeking to enter into the fourth God Question: This means that all loving relationships are, by their very nature, divine stuff. Hence, God's love is intimately and intrinsically intertwined within our human urge to seek love by forming relationships with one another. So our human relationships take us to the core of our humanness, and through them we cross the threshold into the divine essence. Thus the first point we have uncovered with the fourth God Question is that we find God's love in our human relationships of love.

But we are not done with the Trinity's implications because by asking the fourth God Question—"*Where is God's love?*"—we stumble across another rather surprising corollary: God's love is found most directly in human community because we believe in a God whose essence is communal. Since this Triune God is our creator, the doctrine of the Trinity also tells us that we human beings are created in and for community. The very word *community* means "unity with"—a sense of oneness in our plurality. Hence, we are not made as isolated individuals but as social beings bonded together in union with each other and with God through love. Therefore, it is not inappropriate to say that God's love is manifested most tangibly in experiences of community because God is a community.

This explains why I am always somewhat at a loss when I am confronted by a well-meaning friend or even a street-corner stranger who stares intently into my eyes and asks: "Have you accepted Jesus Christ as your personal Lord and Savior?" I usually stammer out awkwardly, "I'm a Catholic." The friend or stranger seems to take this answer as a "no" and proceeds to tell me that I am not saved unless I have a *personal* relationship.

If by *personal relationship* they mean that our salvation is through a person, then I fully agree. After all, Pope Benedict XVI makes this point in his encyclical:

> *We have come to believe in God's love:* in these words the Christian can express the fundamental decision of his life. Being Christian is not the result of an ethical choice or a lofty idea, but the encounter with an event, a person, which gives life a new horizon and a decisive direction. (*DCE* 1)

But it always sounds to me like those Christians who emphasize "my personal relationship with Jesus Christ" are talking about an isolated thing or private connection. Possibly a better response on my part would be: "Well yes, I do have a relationship with the person of Jesus, but your statement is incomplete, as I believe salvation is not an exclusively individual experience, but rather an irreducibly social reality."

Saint Paul first expressed how being in relationship with God involves being dissolved into the unity of community. First, the dissolving part: "Do you not know that all of us who have been baptized into Christ Jesus were baptized into his death? Therefore we have been buried with him by baptism into death, so that, just as Christ was raised from the dead by the glory of the Father, so we too might walk in newness of life....So you also must consider yourselves dead to sin and alive to God in Christ Jesus" (Romans 6:3–4, 11). Paul indicates that our being, our very self, has been ontologically converged *into* Christ by the waters of baptism.

Paul, though, goes a step further: this unity with Christ, this at-one-ness in Christ, this fullness within Christ is not simply a one-to-one relationship but an organic incorporation into the Body of Christ. The classic expression of this Body of Christ theology is in his First Letter to the Corinthians: "For just as the body is one and has many members, and all the members of the body, though many, are one body, so it is with Christ. For in the one Spirit we were all baptized into one body—Jews or Greek, slaves or free—and we were all made to drink of one Spirit.... Now you are the Body of Christ and individually members of it" (12:12–13, 27). While staunchly insisting on the need for a personal encounter with God and the dignity of the individual human person, we Christians must take seriously Paul's image that salvation—that our unity within God's love—has a corporate dimension.

The essentially communitarian nature of faith was expressed by Pope Benedict XVI in this manner:

> Union with Christ is also union with all those to whom he gives himself. I cannot possess Christ just for myself; I can belong to him only in union with all those who have become, or who will become, his own. Communion draws me out of myself towards him, and thus also towards unity with all Christians. We become "one body", completely joined in a single existence. Love of God and love of neighbour are now truly united: God incarnate draws us all to himself (*DCE* 14).

This radical communitarian view of life is startlingly countercultural in our American context. The American mind has been ingrained with a strong belief in individualism because the Founding Fathers' lopsided focus on personal independence was premised on their Protestant religious framework, which stressed a one-to-one relationship to God. Hence, we feel we should be able to "go it alone" and "do it ourselves."

Yet, as the above probing of the fourth God Question reveals, an excessive spirit of individualism is not consistent with our belief in a Trinitarian God, a God whose very essence consists of community: the unity of three persons in one being. Both theologically and practically, we are saved in community. The author of the First Letter of John made this point about the social nature of salvation—which is just fancy shorthand for being manifestly bonded to God through love—in this manner: "Those who say, 'I love God,' and hate their brothers or sisters, are liars; for those who do not love a brother or sister whom they have seen, cannot love God whom they have not seen. The commandment we have from him is this: those who love God must love their brothers and sisters also" (4:20–21). As Saint Ignatius emphasized, love exists more in actions than in words. So the fourth God Question tells us that God's love is directly found through our loving relationships with our brothers and sisters.

And who is my brother and sister? The First Letter of John is unflinching in its assessment: "We know love by this—that he laid down his life for us—and we ought to lay down our lives for one another. How does God's love abide in anyone who has the world's goods and sees a brother or sister in need and yet refuses help? Little children, let us love, not in word or speech, but in truth and action" (3:16–18). The influence of the First Letter of John on Pope Benedict's first encyclical is obvious in his emphasis that Jesus is especially present in the poor: "Love of God and love of neighbour have become one: in the least of the brethren we find Jesus himself, and in Jesus we find God" (*DCE* 15). So, an engagement with the fourth God Question informs us that God's love is found in every loving relationship, but it burns especially fervently in serving the poor.

Most of us find this focus on the poor rather inconvenient. Can't we just stick with familiar family and comfortable companions? Recognizing our resistance to love's demand that we give a preferential option to the poor, Dorothy Day constantly quoted Father Zosima, a character in Fyodor Dostoevsky's novel, *The Brothers Karamazov:* "Love in action is a harsh and dreadful thing compared to love in dreams" (Miller, *A Harsh and Dreadful Love,* 9). Knowing and living in communion with a Triune God is only possible through self-sacrificially loving others, especially those in need. It is that simple. It is that hard. It is that wonderful.

Conversing With Grace

After taking in this beautiful vista, Ryan and I return to our car and drive to our shuttle pickup spot in the prearranged parking lot. After a short wait, a van towing a canoe trailer appears. A young twenty-something woman emerges from the cab, scratching her arm. She looks up with a quirky smile, and says, "Well, my guess is that I am looking for you, and you're looking for me. My name is Grace." With his own smile on his lips, Ryan replies, "I sure hope you're here to pick us up; otherwise we have one heck of a portage in front of us." We exchange introductions, quickly transfer our supplies to the van, and mount our canoe on the trailer.

Our driver has an engaging personality. A few simple questions quickly lead to some interesting and funny stories. How long have you been working for the shuttle service? "This is my first season working here. Ever since high school, I've been working up in Alaska during the summer, doing bike tours for people coming in on cruise ships. Then in winter, I'm a ski instructor in Utah." What made you come to Wisconsin this year? "My grandparents, who live near Boscobel, are getting older. I wanted to spend some time with them before they...Well, they're getting older. I grew up here in Wisconsin, so I thought I should come back to be near them. I'm named after my grandmother." With that last *non sequitur,* she becomes silent.

Searching for new subject matter to move past this weighty pause: What was it like to work in Alaska? "Alaska is amazing. So beautiful. But the work was nasty crazy! These bike tours were down a mountain. Because you are always going downhill, you don't need to pedal much. But we would get people coming on these tours who could barely ride a bike! The nasty crashes they cause were unreal. And then, even though we would do this training beforehand to make sure everyone knew to press the rear brake before they engage the front brake, at least once a week we'd have someone get going too fast, panic, and press the first thing they could, and, *BAM,* catapult themselves over their handle bars. I don't know how many really nasty wounds—you know, with the flesh scraped off to the bone—that I had to bandage up, plucking out gravel and stuff. And some of the broken bones! Bones in the human body ain't supposed to point in the directions I've seen them point. Nasty stuff." One thing is clear: she liked to use the adjective "nasty."

Another question: What's this canoe shuttle job like? "A lot less drama. Well, there was this time that these three guys and one gal rented two canoes for the day. One guy had a broken foot that was in a cast. He could barely get in the boat. The woman was his girlfriend. During their trip, the girl apparently flashed the guys in the other boat. You know, flipped up her bikini top. Well, the broken-leg guy started yelling at her and broke up with her right there. Kicked her out of his canoe and paddled off on his own. So the two guys arrive at the takeout spot with this girl curled up at the bottom of their canoe, crying. We had to pick her up and carry her out. She'd had a lot to drink. But the other guy, well, we waited and waited, but he never showed up. Finally, we had to go find him. He was stranded on an island. With his cast, he had stomped a hole through the fiberglass hull of the canoe. What a bunch of jerks. It was nasty." And so the stories go.

We arrive at Boscobel and unload at the put-in landing. With a wave of her hand, our driver leaves us as Ryan and I begin loading the canoe at the water's edge. We push off, paddling out of the inlet and into the main channel. Easter Rock rises immediately on the other side of the river. This outcropping got its name because early settlers traveled each year in the predawn gloom to this lofty spot, where bracing stone touches wafting heaven, to celebrate the Lord's rising from his cold tomb as the first rays of sunlight reached forth in embracing warmth. Even to this day, a large cross is planted on its rocky shelf. In the light of this sign, we begin the final leg of the Russell River Rendezvous.

Once we settle into a paddling rhythm, Ryan turns and says, "Well, what did you think about our driver's stories?" I respond,

"Colorful, to say the least." "No kidding. Did you notice," Ryan replies, "that all her stories always came around to be about people's misfortunes? Oh, wait, that would be their 'nasty' misfortunes." I chuckle at this last joke and Ryan continues, "She's a nice person, but she seems to see life as a series of disasters hanging around every corner. But maybe that's where she is at now, with her grandparents dying and all. I wonder if she realizes that her words reveal that much about herself." Classic Ryan! Even as a young child, he is able to hear the unstated in the spoken.

Given what we have discovered in relation to the fourth God Question—that God's essential nature is a relationship of love, and hence we are enfolded within God through our relationships of love—then, in a tangible way, our everyday conversations are doorways into the divine presence. Far too often we modern Americans fail to consider the importance of conversation and the power of words. Maybe we have become desensitized to the preciousness of communication because our world is inundated with words flooding from our radios, cell phones, iPods, and televisions. Even more ominously, shock jocks, political pundits, and talk-show hosts seem to dictate the cultural norms for acceptable discourse. As a result, we as a society seem more enthralled with the verbal exchanges between posturing peacocks than with the lyrical nature of poetic prose. Thus, we rarely, if ever, recognize the underlying sacredness of language.

And yet our religious heritage beckons us to see the divine nature of language because communication is the fundamental means of creating and sustaining relationships. Even our English language reflects a primordial understanding about the spiritual power of words. Is not the similarity between the word *conversation* and *conversion* a sign that the sharing of our stories and the discussing of our dreams often transforms our visions of our lived reality? Hence, is it any surprise that Jesus mainly used parables—pithy little stories—to pry open enough space in people's attitudes to allow them to re-turn (which is the literal meaning of *conversion*: to turn again) toward relationship with one another and with God? Here's another example: our words *communication* and *communion* come from the same Latin root. Once again, does this not reveal a profound truth that the common union we create among ourselves through conversation is fundamentally and intrinsically related to our most radical experience of sacramental unity with God?

We see the same respect for the mysteriously divine power of language in the biblical texts. Recall the Creation story in Genesis 1; God creates by uttering words ("*God* said..."). There is an important insight here: our words, our conversations, our communication *do* have the power to create new realities by shaping and explaining our experiences. Even the Hebrew word for *word, dabar,* also has the meaning of "thing" or "deed." Thus, language in the Jewish mind has an active reality to it; words *are* something and they *do* something. So the Hebrew of the Bible tells us that our childhood taunt got it entirely wrong: words hurt just as much...if not more...than sticks and stones because there is a substance to words and words have an effect. In short, words matter.

Certainly this same understanding of language is present in the Koine Greek of the New Testament, for Greek has two words for *word*. One simply means "word," but the other—*logos*—not only means "word," but also means "order," "wisdom," "revelation," and "rational principle." So the Greeks saw language as almost mystical in its power to order our lives according to some higher principle of wisdom or revelation. Once we realize the range of meanings for the word *logos*, then suddenly the significance of the first verse in the Gospel of John leaps out at us: "In the beginning was the Word (*logos*), and the Word (*logos*) was with God, and the Word (*logos*) was God." Since the gospel identifies Jesus as the *logos*, then he is the spirit of wisdom who orders our life according to the divine principle.

So if we sincerely desire to live within the fourth God Question—to allow our daily existence to be infused with God's love—we must train our tongue to speak with more respect and love, as well as avoid rash judgments and uncharitable opinions. Maybe we need to start talking about a second Golden Rule: "...[O]ut of the abundance of the heart the mouth speaks" (Matthew 12:34). Christ's love should flow from our heart so that love emanates from our mouth. If our mouth does not speak love, then there is no love in our hearts. The fourth God Question calls on us to talk to every person as if we are speaking to the very ear of Christ.

This last injunction might sound quite flowery and quixotically idealistic. However, a lawyer friend heard that the secret to Mother Teresa's great love was that she consciously sought to see Christ in each poor, dying person. As she washed crawling maggots from their open-sore wounds, spooned thin soup into their cracked-lipped mouths, and cradled their gangrene-stinking bodies against her own, she actively pictured this person as the very body of Christ, for that is truly what this person is. My friend decided that for Lent he would not give up sweets but do a rather simple thing: each time he greeted another person, he would say to himself "This is Christ" and then try to treat them as such. He reported that it was the hardest Lent of his life because it caused him to revile against his own words and attitudes as he strove to deeply love others. He even said it cost him some money because he wasn't willing to say just anything to win a case. But it was worth the cost because it also changed him. By Christ-centering his words, his soul was re-formed. He became more attentive, more compassionate, more loving.

His story tells us of one place we find God's love: in our own words. We emanate the zeal of the wholehearted life—the life of vibrant love—by becoming conscious of the sacredness of our words, our conversations, and our communication. How we might be transformed if we utter every syllable and each sentence as if they are the word of God! Because in one very real sense, they are; they carry with them the mysterious power of God to effect conversion and create communion. They are the primary conduit of relationship. So if we truly are seeking the fourth God Question, we will bear this divine, precious gift of language with awe and reverence, allowing our words to create a spirit of harmony by speaking love.

If Marquette were with us today, I think he would appreciate this discussion about conversation. Not only was he himself a master of languages, but he had a terrifying firsthand experience of the consequences of not having access to the binding power of words. Marquette's and Jolliet's encounters with the many native bands were all peaceful because they were able to communicate with the tribes along the Mississippi. However, just before they reached the Arkansas River, the failure of words almost proved fatal. You can still hear Marquette's fear in his description of this incident:

> We had recourse to our patroness and guide, the Blessed Virgin Immaculate, whose assistance we certainly needed, for in the distance we could hear the Indians shouting continually to prepare themselves for combat. Armed with bows, arrows, hatchets, clubs, and shields, they made ready to attack us on both land and water. Some of them embarked in great wooden canoes, one party going upriver, the other downriver, in order to intercept us and surround us on all sides. Those who were on land went back and forth, as if to open the attack. In fact, some young men plunged into the water to come and seize my canoe, but the current forced them to return to land. One of them hurled his club, which passed over our heads without striking us. In vain, I showed the calumet and made them signs that we were not coming to make war. The alarm continued, and they were already preparing to pierce us with arrows from all sides when God suddenly touched the hearts of the old men who were standing at the water's edge. No doubt this event came about through the sight of our calumet; they had not recognized it from a

> distance, but as I continued to display it, it finally had an
> effect, and they checked the ardor of their young men....
> There we landed, though not without fear. At first, we
> had to speak by signs, because none of them understood
> the six languages which I spoke. At last, we found an old
> man who could speak a little Illinois. (*JR*, 208)

As always, actions spoke louder than words. The extension
of the calumet, the peace pipe given to him by the Illinois, literally saved their skins. While the breakdown in communication
certainly endangered their lives, the greatest tragedy for Marquette was that the lack of communication prevented a meeting
of souls.

> We informed them...that we were going to the sea. They
> understood us very well, but I know not whether they
> comprehended what I told them about God and about
> matters pertaining to their salvation. This is a seed cast
> onto the ground which will bear fruit in its time....They
> offered us sagamite and fish, and we passed the night
> among them in some anxiety. (*JR*, 208–209)

If conversation is stifled, conversion is thwarted.

I suppose Marquette, as he paddled down the Wisconsin
River, took little notice of the put-in spot where Ryan and I entered
the river, but one of the great efforts at casting seeds through the
Word of God sprouted here. In 1898, two traveling salesmen,
John Nicholson and Samuel Hill, sat huddled together in Room
19 of the Central House Hotel in Boscobel. These two devout
Christians read their Bibles and prayed together as their business
compatriots downed drinks and raised ruckus in the hotel bar.
Gratified by the power of the Word of God to help them journey
faithfully while separated from hearth and home, they resolved to
meet the following year to form an association that would come
to have a very straightforward goal: to place a Bible in every hotel

room in the United States. They named their group after a biblical hero who selected his company based on who drank deeply from the river (see Judges 7:4–7).

And so Gideons International was conceived along the banks of the Wisconsin River. The Gideons now have a quarter of a million members in 181 countries. They distribute an amazing 63,000,000 Bibles each year: an average of one million copies each week, or two per second! And all because two men formed a conspiracy of goodness.

Ah, that's the call of the fourth God Question: create conspiracies of goodness! The word *conspire* literally means "to breathe with" because those in a conspiracy huddle so closely together that they breathe one anothers' breaths. Maybe that is what Genesis 2 is trying to say in describing God as breathing (Hebrew: *ruah*) in the *face* of the human person. And even in Genesis 1, God's *ruah*, which can be translated as breath, spirit, or even wind, is blown on the *face* of the earth. Might all this deep breathing by God be making a point: God desires to form a conspiracy of goodness with us and even with the entire earth. So the fourth God Question leads us to understand that one way we participate in God's Grand Conspiracy of Goodness is by respecting the divine power of the words—sounds formed by our very breaths—that we speak to one another. Communication is a divine gift, for by it we foster relationship with one another and so through it we come into the very core of God's being.

Singing About Grace

It is a cool, sunny afternoon; perfect paddling weather. We also have the river to ourselves, which is not surprising since this western-most section of the river carries, on average, 80 percent less boat traffic. The ideal conditions are matched by the scenery. This stretch from Boscobel to the Mississippi is one of the more picturesque due to a change in the landscape's topology. The glacial waters that burst through the Baraboo Hills thousands of years ago initially encountered soft sandstone. But around Muscoda, those glacial torrents started running into limestone. As the water cut through this hard rock, it sculpted some impressive precipices.

Given the inviting weather, the peaceful setting, and the dramatic surroundings, Ryan and I are in no rush on this day. For this leg of the journey, I purchased a book on the birds of Wisconsin. So we often allow the current to carry us as we use our binoculars to do some bird watching. We are well rewarded with numerous sightings of bald eagles, both adults and juveniles. We stop counting after fourteen. More than once we even drift directly underneath an eagle perched on a dead tree's outstretched branch.

Our national symbol has made quite a recovery in recent years along the lower Wisconsin River. Bald eagles were nearly extinct because of the agricultural use of pesticides (like DDT) in the 1950s. The DDT ran off the fields and into the rivers, infecting the fish, which were then consumed by bald eagles. The DDT physiologically inhibited the eagles from producing eggshells thick enough to protect the conceived chicks. Eagle populations plummeted. For example, there were only eighty-two breeding pairs of bald eagles in all of Wisconsin in 1972. In that same year, a federal law banned the use of DDT and the eagles started a slow but steady comeback.

The dramatic turnaround in the fate of the eagles is evident along the lower Wisconsin. During the previous summer, the state Department of Natural Resources counted 614 bald eagles along this 100-mile stretch of the river. That is an amazing number considering that there were only twenty-two bald eagles in this same area as late as 1992. As a result of its rebound across the United States, the bald eagle was removed from the federal Endangered Species list in the summer of 2007. This is certainly a story of hope and regeneration.

Ryan is quite informed about the environmental history of the effect of DDT on fish populations and bald eagles from his college biology class. So we talk of this and many other things as we travel lazily down the river. We fall into a gentle pattern: paddle briefly, drift leisurely, observe keenly. After a while, Ryan starts singing an impromptu song, spontaneously creating the lyrics. With each lyric, I laugh at Ryan's turn of a phrase. Not that I'm surprised. Ryan has regaled the family with this talent for years. He often takes an incident that has just happened and creates a musical rendition on the spot.

Ryan's musical talent extends beyond a nice singing voice and a quick wit for lyrics. He plays the piano, guitar, and drums with great skill, but all by ear. After years of lessons, his piano teacher was shocked one day to discover that Ryan did not know how to read music. It was this teacher's practice to introduce any new piece of music by first playing the music for the student. Ryan would listen and then he would reproduce it while assiduously staring at the notes on the sheet, but actually following the melody in his memory. To this day, he does not know how to read much music...he simply plays what is within him.

And that seems to work. Last Christmas, he asked for a clarinet because he wanted to add a wind instrument to his repertoire. That afternoon, he watched the accompanying DVD to figure out how to put the clarinet together but then turned it off when it moved into the playing instructions. He went to his bedroom, tootingly experimenting with the sounds. He re-emerged about two hours later to play his first tune. No, it was not "Twinkle, Twinkle Little Star," but rather "Gabriel's Oboe," the soundtrack to the movie *The Mission*—a rather complex piece!

My guess is that Ryan's insightfulness into people's souls and his innate ability to play by ear stem from the same quality: he attentively listens for the patterns in the sounds. It strikes me that

Marquette had this same characteristic. His journal is full of careful observations about the flora and fauna of the landscape, the characteristics and behaviors of the wildlife, and the culture and personality of the native tribes. It is especially interesting to see how Marquette looks for the good in the native people he encounters while traveling down the Mississippi.

Maybe Marquette's attentiveness to the created patterns came from his Jesuit training. In his discussion of a prayer exercise in the *Spiritual Exercises* called the "Contemplation on the Love of God," Saint Ignatius advises us to "consider how God works and labors for me in all things created on the face of the earth—that is, behaves like one who labors—as in the heavens, elements, plants, fruits, cattle, etc., giving them being, preserving them, giving them vegetation and sensation, etc. Then to reflect on myself" (Fleming, *Draw Me Into Your Friendship*, 178). Now *that* is an image: visualizing God as a mother in labor, continually birthing all that is created. In Romans 8:23, Paul was bold enough when he describes the whole of creation groaning in labor pains, but Saint Ignatius, knowing that God is in all things, calls us to see the deep-down thing of our loving God wombfully laboring in a continual action of creating. And all out of love for us.

Saint Ignatius is describing (in much more metaphorical language) something that Saint Thomas Aquinas had said long before him. Using philosophical terminology, Aquinas put it this way: Everything in the world—all material existence—only exists because it is caused (that is, created) by something else. Hence, nothing exists that is not caused or created. However, there cannot be an infinite regression of causes as there has to be, logically speaking, something outside the chain of causes that started this process. By implication, therefore, there must have been something which was beyond existence and beyond time—which was, is, and will be—that initiated this process of existence. In Aquinas' terminology, there must have been an Uncaused Cause that initiated—and continually initiates—existence and time. This Uncaused Cause is what we call God. As the source of time and existence, God is beyond time and existence. There is no past, present, or future time in God. There is only *IS*. There is no nonexistence or existence in God. There is only *BEING*.

We should not confuse the Uncaused Cause with the big bang. The big bang theory does not explain who or what created the gases that exploded to start the creation of our universe. The Uncaused Cause is that which created those gases (or the process that resulted in those gases) and hence caused the big bang and was in the big bang.

What does all this have to do with the fourth God Question: *Where is God's love?* Everything! We know through our unique human consciousness of time about the true origin of existence, so we are able to perceive a startling fact: our very existence is only possible because of our absolute dependence on and ultimate origin in that which surpasses time and existence: that is, God. Stated more succinctly, our being is fundamentally connected with the Ultimate Reality. In fact, the very etymology of the word *existence* makes this point clear: our life is "out of IS" (Latin: *ex* = out of; *ist* = is). We come from, we derive of, we live in That Which Is.

Cool, yes, but now for the punch line: this means that every breath we take, every minute that passes, every seed that sprouts—*everything*—ultimately depends on God's choice to continue to labor—to extend his very Being through Existence—to the created world. If God ever stops extending God's gift of life, then the entire universe would vanish…disappear…cease. But remember: God is love. So every extension of That Which Is into the created order is an act of love. Hence, creation exists, and continues to exist, because God continues to love that which God creates. So life only is because God loves. We can say, in effect, that love is the DNA of the universe. So Ignatius is absolutely right: every ray of the sun, every chirp of a bird, every wiggle of a worm manifests an ongoing labor of love, the wombful love of God.

Recognizing God's loving presence in creation leads us to one of those "slap the forehead with the palm" moments. For here is a rather obvious place where we can find God's love: by relishing nature! If not just human beings, but all of creation exists through God's continual extension of God's Being, then a relationship with nature is an experience of God's love. While human are especially made in God's image, *all* created things exist because they have a relationship with our Triune God. God creates as God is, and God is relationship. Thus all things exist in relationship. And if we enter into relationship, we enter into God's Trinitarian love. So, again, the fourth God Question tells us that we discover, and are *called to discover*, God's love by forming a relationship with nature.

If that isn't enough, there is more to consider. Did you notice that after Ignatius calls on us to consider God's laboring action in creation, he adds a rather enigmatic phrase: "Then to reflect on myself." What does that mean? It's not even a complete sentence. I wonder if Saint Francis de Sales, who was trained by the Jesuits, did not grasp the inner power of Ignatius' cryptic injunction when he wrote:

> Consider the eternal love which God has had for you. Before our Lord, as man, suffered for you on the Cross, as God, he knew and loved you in his infinite goodness. When did he begin to love you? When he began to be God? No, for he is without beginning and without end; he has always been God and so has loved you from eternity and in that love prepared all the graces and favors he has bestowed on you. He tells you so through the Prophet Jeremiah in words addressed to you as though there were no one else: "With an everlasting love, I have love you, and now in mercy I have drawn you to myself" (Jeremiah 31:3). Among other things he thought of drawing you to make your resolutions to serve him. (Saint Francis de Sales, *Introduction to the Devout Life*, 256)

We are loved eternally. Not just now. Not just in the future. But in the past. *The eternal past.* Before you were baptized and even before you were born, God loved you and prepared for you. Before your parents existed and even before the species *Homo sapiens* evolved, God loved you and prepared for you. Before the dinosaurs and even before the earth was formed from a molten mass, God loved you and prepared for you. Before the big bang and even before the existence of time, God loved you and prepared for you. So what shall we do in return for this astounding love?

Each of us needs to examine that last question in relation to our personal lives. It's a hefty consideration, but the crisis of our era demands that we as a community also address this question in relation to the natural environment, which, like us, exists through God's daily labor pains. If the great environmental question for our nation in the 1970s was whether we could change our use of chemicals to save our national symbol from extinction, the question in these "aught" years is far more momentous and imperative. Today our challenge is not the survival of a species but literally of the very environment itself. Global warming is no longer a hypothesis or a theory but a fact and a reality (see United Nations, "Climate Change," 2007). Science has proven it beyond debate: we are literally killing off the world by our lifestyle choices that spew chemicals into the atmosphere. Terrifyingly, we are altering creation's childbirthing groans into death-knelling gasps as our universe chokes for breath.

The situation is dire, but there is hope. We can point to the rebirth of the bald eagle as proof that we can muster the national will to resolve environmental problems through effective laws, even when those laws require significant changes in how we organize our economic life. Candidly, though, the changes demanded of us to reverse global warming are much more intimidating because they require altering practices that are much more tightly woven into the fabric of our social and economic lives. We will need much greater national resolve to resuscitate the earth's atmosphere than at any other point in our history.

Nonetheless, we still have hope because we have the promise of the resurrection. We do not tackle this problem alone. The God of New Life is laboring right alongside us. Let's accept God's invitation to form a conspiracy of goodness by changing our choices that literally stifle the laboring breaths of God in creation. In these aught years, it's time to do what we ought. Let's get started loving what we are called to love—and we are called to love what God loves. And God loves his Creation; let's care for what God loves. The fourth God Question demands it of us.

Firing Up Grace

Ryan and I journey down the river at this leisurely pace until late afternoon. As we approach the mouth of the Little Kickapoo Creek, Ryan asks, "Hey, Dad, you want to stop and camp here? This looks like a good fishing spot." Ryan is probably the best fisherman of our four sons, so I listen to his assessment of good fishing habitat. Stopping now allows us to set up camp, eat dinner, and then spend the evening fishing.

We check out the sandbar island across from the creek. While I look to see if there is a good location for our tent, Ryan explores the fishing potential. "This channel between the island and the shore looks promising, Dad. There is a sharp drop-off about ten feet from the island's shore." There is also a good supply of firewood available on the island. So it is settled. We unpack the canoe and establish camp.

While I start a fire so we can roast our bratwursts, Ryan tries his fishing luck along the island's shoreline. Unfortunately, Ryan doesn't have any bites before dinner. Nonetheless, we enjoy a delicious meal. Food always has a more intense flavor when eaten on a sandy beach after a warm day of paddling on a river.

However, we don't linger over our dinner. Rather we load the canoe with our fishing gear and paddle to likely looking fishing locations. We try next to submerged trees, the island's point, spots shaded from overhanging branches, and the confluence of the creek with the river. We paddle a little up the creek, and then try fishing while drifting down into the river. Not a single bite. We fish past twilight and into the night, but to no avail.

We finally concede to the fickle fish and head back to the campsite. We take consolation in a large fire, roasted marshmallows, and s'mores. We have a wonderful, heart-to-heart conversation about the promise and meaning of life. It is one of those interactions that John Henry Cardinal Newman (1801–1890) would have described as *cor ad cor loquitur*—"heart speak[ing] to heart." Newman was the quintessential academic, but he adopted this expression as his motto because he knew that knowledge about God cannot and should not be confined by what we can say about God with the mind. He warned against those who asserted religious certainty strictly on the basis of rational arguments or authoritative pronouncements. A true, authentic, and healthy faith must engage the *whole* person: intellect, affect, and will. So our whole self—our heart—must be engaged in the conversation of faith. We only hear God's heart speaking to us when we reveal our whole self to God and to others.

In the course of our fireside discussion, we talk about Ryan's early years. During that time, Stephanie and I were working at a Jesuit high school, Red Cloud Indian School, on the Pine Ridge Indian Reservation in western South Dakota. Ryan was born in the middle of the night in the midst of a prairie snowstorm. It took almost two hours to drive the forty-five miles through the empty plains landscape on treacherous, ice-slick roads to the local hospital—arriving just before Ryan emerged from the womb! Happily, our doctor, traversing the snow-drifted roads on cross-country skis, walked into the labor room just in time to catch Ryan.

After I recount the story of his harrowing birth, Ryan says, "You know, when I was in grade school, I used to think I was Lakota Sioux because I was born on the reservation." I start to laugh and Ryan responds, "Hey, it wasn't funny. I told all my friends. The teacher would ask me what it was like to be a Native American. I was known as the Indian kid." Now I am laughing even harder. Unfazed, Ryan continues, "Man, you wouldn't believe how embarrassed I was when one of the teachers, in front of the whole class, told me that I was not Native American. That she asked my parents and that you told her that I was three-fifths Irish and two-fifths Swedish. I was crushed." Now, I suppose I should have stopped laughing at this point, but Ryan's deadpan tone indicates that he thinks this story is a hoot too.

We begin to talk about other family experiences on the reservation. The conversation moves to a discussion about the Lakota religion, especially the Sun Dance. In this ceremony, the dancer's skin is pierced and a piece of wood is embedded under the skin. A leather thong is tied to the wood and, in turn, to a cottonwood tree. The pierced dancer then dances, pulling the leather thong taut from time to time until a patch of his skin eventually rips away, freeing the embedded wood.

I once asked a Holy Man about the meaning of the skin piercing at the Sun Dance. As a man well versed in the ways of the River, he answered with a question: "Were you born in a bank bag?" Smiling at my very puzzled face, the Holy Man continued, "You Christians give your money as an offering to God, but all we can give back to the Great Spirit is that which he has given us—our flesh. We Lakota give our flesh because that is all we came into the world with and that is all we will leave with—it is the only thing we have that is truly us." I found the Holy Man's words quite insightful and very profound.

At the same time, even this flesh offering is, ultimately, incomplete. We humans are not simply flesh. We are also made of spirit. Further, we are beings created in and to love, and love is an activity because it is mainly about giving. Giving inherently expresses a person's aliveness, because all a person can truly give in love is himself or herself. The giving of one's self means the giving of one's life—our most precious "possession." We give to others what is thriving in ourselves: our joy, humor, knowledge, sadness, love—all of which are expressions of that which is alive in us. Therefore, giving is an exquisite joy because it is a life-giving activity. As a result, one could say that something is born in the act of giving, something is birthed. Love is birthed.

However, our character determines the degree to which we can give of ourselves. As Saint Ignatius emphasized in the *Spiritual Exercises*, the ability to love depends on our freedom to love, and our freedom depends on the degree that we have formed our whole self—intellect, affect, and will—to emulate Christ's model of love. This is why so many of the saints stress the development of the virtues, that is, Christ's values, in living the spiritual life. The key virtue that we must instill within us is Christ's generosity, his self-giving love. If we do this, we become transformed from people who seek the fourth God Question to people who live in the fourth God Question.

Living in the fourth God Question is work because generosity is work; it requires hard effort. We already often feel overwhelmed by the daily work necessary just to function in life, so we fear that we do not have the energy required to love fully those around us. Thus, it is easier to allow our old, wooden patterns to stay embedded in our lives: watch the TV, snap at the children, ignore the spouse, bury ourselves in work. Instead of entering into the dance of life, we hoard our time, feelings, and wisdom, giving only out of our excess. But Christ's love calls us to enter into the dance—to pull away from the anesthetizing routine and become startling, even painfully, free to respond to the needs and lives of those we are called to love.

The fourth God Question beckons us to enter the dance by facing this challenge every day: how much of myself am I willing to give to my spouse, children, parents, coworkers, and friends today? Am I able to respond with a generous spirit to others' important demands and petty annoyances? What will be my posture toward the world; will I greet it with an extended open hand or a cocked closed fist? Am I willing to be like Christ, willing to empty myself into the world? These are frightening steps, but we must enter the dance ring in faith, knowing that Christ's powerful hand will grasp ours, twirl us, and uphold us as we dance the dance of life. Let us dance the *Son* Dance!

Our conversation continues to swirl from topic to topic, but after a while Ryan and I fall silent as we stare into the fire. But even this stillness contains a conversation. While there is a convergence between conversation and conversion, I wonder how many conversions really occur as a result of well-reasoned arguments or tightly constructed propositions? Maybe some, but it seems more often the case that significant transformations in our lives are the result of encounters with images. We humans are moved by pictures, objects, stories, and actions much more than by disembodied words.

Two examples from Marquette's life dramatize this point. First, he reports in his first encounter with the Illinois that the tribe's chief "begged us on behalf of all his nation not to go farther, on account of the great dangers to which we would expose ourselves. I replied that I feared not death and that I believed there was no greater happiness than that of losing my life for the glory of Him who has made all. This is what these poor people cannot understand" (*JR*, 199). Maybe they did not understand Marquette's words about the Christian God, but they heard the attraction of his fearless self-giving by journeying forward. Might it be that Marquette's actions spoke to their hearts, and it was this that motivated them, as Marquette later reports, to enjoin him to come back and teach them about the Christian faith?

We have already seen the second example from Marquette's life of the conversionary power of images. When Marquette and his band were almost slaughtered by the tribe north of the Arkansas River, it was the power of an image, the calumet, that turned the hearts of their attackers from war to peace. Marquette's journal offers a lengthy description of the Illinois' customs, beliefs, and lifestyle, and then he wraps up his narrative with a discussion of the calumet.

> There remains no more, except to speak of the calumet. There is nothing more mysterious or more respected among them. Less honor is paid to the crowns and scepters of kings than the Indians bestow upon this object. It seems to be the god of peace and of war, the arbiter of life and of death. It has but to be carried upon one's person and displayed to enable one to walk safely through the midst of enemies, who, in the heat of battle, will lay down their arms when it is shown. For that reason, the Illinois gave me one, to serve as a safeguard among all the nations through whom I had to pass during my voyage....It is fashioned from a red stone, polished like marble, and bored in such a manner that one end serves as a receptacle for the tobacco, while the other fits into the stem. The stem is a piece of wood two feet long, as thick as an ordinary cane, and bored through the middle. It is ornamented with the heads and necks of various birds of gorgeous plumage, and all along its length are attached long red, green, and other colors. They have a great regard for it, because they look upon it as the calumet of the sun, and, in fact, they offer it to the latter to smoke when they wish to obtain a calm, or rain, or fine weather. (*JR*, 202)

Marquette then continues to describe the intricate calumet dance that the tribe performed as part of the bestowal ceremony.

Marquette's description makes it clear that the tribe bestowed the calumet on *him*, not the band of voyageurs. Perhaps they singled out Marquette because they recognized him as the holy man of the group, but it also seems that his example of self-giving sacrifice drew the Illinois to respond to him with a gift of protection. Image responded to image.

Maybe this extraordinary interaction between Marquette

and the Illinois is not surprising, since images have the immediate ability to attract and impress our imaginations. The divine gift of the imagination is the portal through which we see beyond the present and experience the wondrous, the door by which we push past the possible to the astonishing. In fact, Jesus conveyed the essence of his message by using an image: the in-breaking of the kingdom of God—an image of what the world *could* be if faith and justice reigned in the world.

Of the three persons of the Trinity, the Holy Spirit seems the most disembodied, the least "imaginable." Certainly the figure of a father is very familiar to each of us. Similarly, we can craft numerous likenesses of Jesus Christ since he became human. However, with the Holy Spirit, we get a dove. A dove? I don't know about you, but the image of a dove is not the most powerful image to be impressed on my imagination!

However, the Acts of the Apostles offers another image: "When the day of Pentecost had come, they were all together in one place. And suddenly from heaven there came a sound like the rush of a violent wind, and it filled the entire house where they were sitting. Divided tongues, as of fire, appeared among them, and a tongue rested on each of them. All of them were all filled with the Holy Spirit and began to speak in other languages, as the Spirit gave them ability" (2:1–4).

The Holy Spirit as the tongues of fire. This is a bit better; we have visceral experiences of fire. Not only have we each had primal experiences of campfires, but we are constantly surrounded by fire. The very light of our world, both during the day and the night, is the result of the sun's fire. But even further, "fire" is contained in each electrical outlet, every light fixture, the engine of each running car, and on and on. Ours is a world charged with energy—an energy that consists of firing electrons and igniting gases. That is an image that can enliven the imagination: the Triune God is enmeshed within the smallest agitation of electrons or even the most unremarkable spark!

This insight takes us to another level of meaning in this story about tongues of fire received in the context of community. The notable part is not the appearance of fire but that the *tongues rested upon each disciple's head.* Since our very thoughts are the result of electrons firing within our brain, then our very brains are, in a very real way, tongues of fire! Since our mind directs our bodily actions, then our very movements are ultimately governed by the power—the spark—of God. Let's not forget that our tongues also are governed by those firing mental electrons—tongues that can speak words of love to each other in response to God's love. In fact, while it is common to interpret the disciples' "speaking in tongues" as representing nonsensible utterances, is it not more likely that this indicates that they were now able to speak more fluently in the language of love that creates relationship? After all, the *Spirit* gives them these utterances, and the Spirit's language is the language of God's loving presence in the world.

So the Holy Spirit is not invisible electricity hidden behind walls nor an inaccessible sun in the distant sky, but rather is present in every loving touch extended to the hurting, every comforting word expressed to the suffering, every tangible action taken to help the needy. That is a powerful image: the Holy Spirit sets our souls ablaze with love for others.

The fourth God Question informs us that the blessing of Pentecost is that we have the opportunity to have our imaginations transformed by the image of the Holy Spirit. The image of the Holy Spirit re-turns our hearts to the Triune God, a relational God who taught us through the Incarnated Word that the essence of the Divine Spirit is made real in the world when we humans embody these three simple words: love one another.

Awakening to Grace

It is early. Too early. At least an hour before Ryan and I had planned to get up for the day. We were going to sleep until 7:00

AM. But a fisherman has another objective: to be at his favorite fishing spot, which apparently is directly across the river from our campsite, at the crack of dawn. So his motorboat roars up the river...at 6:00 AM. He achieves his goal; I do not accomplish mine.

However, as I lie in the cool morning with unanticipated alertness and unplanned time, there is a pleasantness to the moment. When the fisherman cuts his motor, the swaying sound of the rolling waves washing against the shore, caused by the boat's wake, has an enveloping rhythm. As these sounds diminish, the bright music of the morning birds filters tenderly into the tent. I relish in that certain lightness that accompanies the beginning of glorious summer days—the kind of delight that comes with entering the day without a time-pressing agenda or overexpansive needs. So my initial semi-conscious curses directed toward our early-arriving fishing neighbor mellow into an awakened sense of gratitude for the greatness of life that God has given us.

I utter a simple prayer, a line from Ephesians that Scripture scholars identify as one of the earliest songs sung at Christian liturgies. It's a resurrection hymn:

> "Sleeper, awake!
> Rise from the dead
> and Christ will shine on you" (5:14).

In other words, wake up and remember God! Too often we fail to recognize that our very existence is completely dependent on God. This is one reason that Saint Ignatius stresses in the *Spiritual Exercises* that the first act of any prayer session should be to become conscious of the presence of God right now and right here. This awareness of the Divine Other is like the tender glances exchanged between lovers. After all, the first step in falling in love is to notice the movements of the other person—the way he or she smiles, pushes back a lock of hair, holds a glass, engages a conversation. So the first step in prayer is to allow God to woo us by beginning to notice the movements of our lover...that is, by noticing God's presence in all things.

I look over at my second son, who bears my name as his middle name. His sleeping face is aglow, bathed in the blessing of the shimmering dawn light. The glory of God shining through the in-breaking sunrise brings to mind a poem, entitled "My Sun," that my own father wrote. It talks about the bright sun but implies the divine Son. As his own son, I wonder if I also hear the echo of my own presence in some of my father's lines.

Oh great source of light, of heat and strength;
You shower down upon me your mighty
beam of warmth.

Where is your source, your first, your essence?
Where do I turn for a glimpse of your beginning?

Would it be in the blue sky above,
Or in the blackness of night,
Wrapped in the mystery of things unseen?

I worry not about such things, for to me
You are as regular as my breadth,
or the beat of my heart.

You are slow and purposeful as you rise each morn,
Reaching out to each object, with unfailing warmth.

You are as gentle as a misty cloud,
As inviting as an open door,
As nourishing as food itself.

Yet, you are hot, intense and fiery;
You are fierce and unrelenting when
you reach down close,
And wring the moisture from around my world.

You seem to care not about the power of your touch,
For many the time you burned me,
*   as I entrusted my body to you.*

Hear this not as unhappiness; hear it more as respect;
For the gift you share with all, and the life you beget.

I dare not dream of a future time,
when your light will no longer shine,
When the earth around me grows cold,
*   and life is left behind.*

But only then will I be sure that you were meant to be,
A vital part of my new life, about to be set free.

My dad's poem seems almost a prayer, as it reflects a consciousness of God's energy in all things. Everything has something of the divine in it because every movement and each moment depends on God infusing existence into it. And God does all this out of love—love for us and for creation. Living in the resurrection means living in love. Christ's resurrection, which Saint Ignatius made the focus of the fourth and final "week" or movement of the *Spiritual Exercises*, is about awakening to the wonder and joy of this God-given life. All of life is a blessing because existence and creation both come from God. As the God of life, God is everywhere, for existence itself exists only in God. As the God of creation, God is in everything, for God formed the material world and brought it into existence.

Fishing for Grace

As the sun's rays intensify, Ryan awakens. When we emerge from the tent, our fishing neighbor is considerate. He starts his boat and motors around the bend so that we have the river's morning to ourselves.

Over breakfast I ask Ryan, "Do you want to see if our luck changes this morning and try fishing around here again?" Ryan munches his Pop-Tart silently as he ponders my question. Then he inquires, "Did our fisherman friend catch anything this morning?" I respond, "I don't know. I didn't hear any sounds like he had a bite." Ryan looks at me with a mischief smile, "And what, pray tell, does it *sound* like when a fish bites on a hook underwater?" Snickering, I answer, "You know what I mean. I didn't hear any splashing water caused by a fighting fish. So I would say the answer is 'no, he did not catch anything.' " "Well," Ryan says as he stretches and lets out a loud yawn, "maybe he wasn't just being charitable when he saw us get up. Maybe he was getting skunked." With this assessment, we decide to pack up and return to our journey down the river.

I am somewhat pleased that we are getting a jump on the paddling. After all, this is a big day: we will be entering the Mississippi River. The goal of this four-stage journey on the River of Discovery is almost achieved.

As the morning progresses, the clear, crisp sky slowly turns to gray as clouds move in from the west. These are not large thunderheads but rather steel-drab clouds that form a misty ceiling just above the trees. When we later stop on a sandbar island for an early lunch, there is a definite threat of rain. As we sit in our collapsible chairs to enjoy our sandwiches, fruit, and cookies, large ploppy raindrops begin to smatter us, forming little craters when they plunk in the dry sand. I dash to the canoe and pull out a large blue tarp. We drape it over ourselves as we sit encased in plastic as we eat our meal.

Happily, this scattered rain shower passes fairly quickly so we can emerge from our blue cocoon. We decide to spend some time fishing, hoping (vainly, it turns out) that this damp weather might pass. I head to the south side to see if there is any action in the channel between us and the neighboring island. Ryan tries an inlet located on the west side of the island.

Soon I hear a loud shout. Ryan's pole is severely bent as he struggles mightily to reel in a large northern pike. I dash back just as Ryan has brought the monster to within three feet of the shore. And then, the fish spits out the hook. Ryan's pole snaps back, the line goes slack. Ryan groans and then shouts, "I can't believe that! How could that fish not be hooked?"

Staring in the water, Ryan exclaims, "Hey, there he is!" Sure enough, the fish is resting about ten feet from shore. Ryan yells, "I'm not done with you fish!" He casts his Dardevle lure toward the spot and starts reeling in the line. The pike follows until it is just three feet from shore and then it stops. It returns to its original bed. Ryan casts again, the northern gives chase, but then halts and swims back. This process is repeated time and again. Sometimes the fish follows but other times it ignores the lure as it glides past its nose.

At one point, Ryan turns and says, "Dad, this fish is doing this on purpose. It's playing me for a fool!" I laugh, but Ryan turns serious. "No, really. When it stops chasing the lure, I swear it looks up at me before it heads back. It really *is* playing me!" "Maybe," I offer helpfully, "it is trying to play *with* you. Maybe it just wants a friend!" Ryan gives me a Dad-I-am-too-old-for-this-playground-morality-lesson look.

I suppose my comment is a bit useless. After all, there is a distinct difference between the fish's and Ryan's behavior: free will. In fact, an intense engagement with the fourth God Question reveals that the gift of free will is, in some ways, the penultimate expression of God's love for us. God's presence is channeled through our human freedom, and it is only because we are free that we are even able to love. Love is possible to the degree to which we are able to give ourselves freely to the other as gift. So *agape love,* that self-giving love that underpins Jesus' supreme act of love, requires freedom.

I can remember a very distinct moment in my life when I thought I had made my first big "free" decision. As my ignominious junior-high career was coming to a pimply, testosterone-challenged end, I felt that I needed to start afresh in high school. I knew what I had to do: quit playing the alto saxophone. Now, I have mentioned Ryan's musical talent. He certainly got that from his mother, not me. My saxophone playing was awful, and it didn't seem to have much cache with the ladies.

With some trepidation, I informed my parents that I did not want to play in the band in high school. To my relief, my parents said I was free to make my own decision. I was free! I thus approached my final end-of-the-year school concert with great joy. The moment was not lost on me as our junior-high band burst into a rendition of "Born Free." As I blew out each note with great gusto, I shouted within myself a proclamation of my own freedom—freedom from the tyranny of ever having to play the saxophone again.

Too often, though, we get trapped in an unreflective, inadequate "American" equation of freedom with the power of choice ("doing whatever I want" or "doing what feels good"). More accurate is Lord Acton's statement that liberty is "not the power of doing what we like, but the right of being able to do what we ought" (quoted in Dulles, "John Paul II and the Truth About Freedom," 37). True freedom comes with transcending individual or group self-interest by knowing what is truly good and then choosing to do the good. Since we are created by a good God, then our very nature disposes us to choose what we perceive to be good for us. The incarnated core of our being calls us to goodness, and thus to God's own self, through our human freedom. Thus if we know the good, but do not choose it, we are not free at all because we have rejected to be true to our authentic, free self in the name of easy convenience, personal gain, or some other false god.

The beauty of freedom is that it says that God desires our happiness, and God accomplishes this end by implanting within us a desire for goodness. As the Jesuit theologian Avery Cardinal Dulles put it: "The truly free person is one who does what is good out of love for goodness itself" (Dulles, 37–38). True liberty must be equated with love. So the grass and wind—nor that playful northern pike—are not truly free because they cannot love. Only humans can be free for, of all God's creatures, only they can love.

Thus, we are born free, but only as free as the *human* grows. We are free to love.

Personally, I think God's choice to give us humans free will was quite risky: we have used it time and again to reject God and harm each other. However, God evidently thought love was worth the peril. That is amazing: God is willing to suffer our rejection because he delights so much in our feeble love. What a sign of God's effusive love! So the fourth God Question truly alerts us that God's loving presence is manifest in the gift of free will. Let us use it properly to love well.

Entering in Grace

We return to the river with Ryan never landing his trophy fish. The weather never clears. At times it lightly sprinkles, but mostly it is just overcast. Nevertheless, my spirit quickens as the current strengthens the nearer we come to the convergence of the Wisconsin and the Mississippi. Not only is the river getting swifter, but it also is wider. The pace quickens. We weave through a last series of islands. To our left, we see the overlook where we took in this marvelous image of the rivers' merging on the previous day. We have been woven in the fabric of God's grandeur.

The river swings around a bend and we see imposing bluffs barring our way in the distance. They mark the western bank of the Mississippi. We are getting close! A wedged-shaped island stands between us and the Mississippi, obscuring our view of its waters. More deep paddling, energized by the moment. We pass this final island by following the channel on the right. As we breach the island's northern-most point, we see the Mississippi before us.

Hard strokes, fast current, quickening hearts. Suddenly the current gently swings our canoe to the left, toward the south. We have arrived at the point of confluence. We are now being borne by the Father of Waters.

I remember being disappointed when I first read Marquette's description of this momentous occasion in his journal. All he had to say was this: "After proceeding forty leagues on this route, we arrived at the mouth of our river, and at forty-two and a half degrees of latitude, we safely entered the Mississippi on the seventeenth of June, with a joy that I cannot express" (*JR*, 194). That's it. No great fanfare. No emotional fireworks. No profound oration. He doesn't even inform us at this point in the narrative about the name he bestows on this new watercourse: "River of the Conception" in honor of Mary's immaculate conception and the conception of God's son within her womb.

I now understand Marquette's subdued reaction. Such joyful moments are better reverenced in stillness. It is my intuition, though, that Marquette uttered a prayer in gratitude to God when he reached this convergence of his desires and God's will. It's possible that he recited the Lord's Prayer or a Hail Mary, but my guess is that he prayed the Suscipe Prayer. This great prayer, which Saint Ignatius wrote as part of the fourth week or movement of the *Spiritual Exercises*, encapsulates the whole of Ignatian spirituality:

> *Take, Lord, and receive all my liberty,*
> *my memory, my understanding*
> *and my entire will,*
> *All I have and call my own.*
>
> *You have given all to me.*
> *To you, Lord, I return it.*
>
> *Everything is yours; do with it what you will.*
> *Give me only your love and your grace.*
> *That is enough for me.* (Fleming, *Draw Me Into Your Friendship*, 177)

Ryan and I, on the other hand, give out a triumphal yell and a celebratory whoop. The personality of the Mighty Mississippi is certainly rawer than the meandering River of Discovery. The current is stronger and the water darker. Our fragility on this powerful river is accentuated when the large barges, loaded with commerce, plow through the water, creating momentous rolling wakes that precariously rock our little canoe. We must turn the canoe to head directly into the waves to prevent capsizing. Yes, the Father of Waters throbs with a force that is awe-ful—both foreboding and inspiring at the same time.

In his lifetime, Marquette never did reach the Immense Waters, the sea, by following the Father of Waters. Once it became evident that the Mississippi emptied into the Gulf of Mexico and that the short distance between the Arkansas River and the sea was controlled by tribes allied with the Spanish, Marquette reports, "Monsieur Jolliet and I held our own council to deliberate upon what we should do—whether we should push on or remain content with the discovery which we had made" (JR, 210). Discerning that "we had obtained all the information that could be desired in regard to this discovery" (JR, 211), they turn their canoes around on July 17, 1673—exactly one month after they had entered the Mississippi River.

Was Marquette disappointed that they stopped so tantalizing short of the sea? Was the journey worth it if they did not arrive at the Immense Waters? Marquette's final words in his journal point to a greater reality than his own:

Had this voyage resulted in the salvation of even one soul, I would consider all my troubles well rewarded, and I have reason to presume that such is the case. For, when I was returning, we passed through the Illinois of the Peouarea [sic], and during three days I preached the faith in all their cabins; after which, while we were embarking, a dying child was brought to me at the water's edge and I baptized it shortly before it died, through an admirable act of providence for the salvation of that innocent soul. (Donnelly, *Marquette*, 229)

Our theology might have changed somewhat from Marquette's day, but our baptismal hope has not. It was on the stream of this hope that Marquette, with his final expelled breath on May 18, 1674, completed his ultimate journey on the Father of Waters to the Immense Waters.

It begins to rain shortly after we enter the Mississippi, so we complete the last three miles down the Mississippi to our final destination awash with water. It is a good omen, a sign of God's overflowing grace. We end this journey not just on water, but within it. How fitting, for ours is a God of superabundant love! Saint Augustine, in the *City of God*, spoke of the "plentitude" of God. While we as humans would probably have been content with just one or two species of flowers, observes Augustine, we have a God so effusive that God created a world brimming with flowers of all different shapes and colors. Ours is a Triune God overflowing with love and creativity, a God of endless waters of rebirth.

God's effusiveness, though, does not stop with creation, time, and existence. It continues beyond all this, for the river leads to the Immense Water of eternal life. We ultimately are all part of something complete because we are drawn into the ubiquitous fullness of All Being through the wonderful, miraculous grace of God's everlasting love for us.

Ryan and I reach the takeout spot. We beach the canoe and then step ashore. My legs buckle and wobble as I step on the shore. I look over at Ryan and say, "I still have my sea legs!" What a gift! I hope I never lose them. But just to be sure, we must continue to journey with the God Questions on the River of Discovery until that time that we are carried by the Father of Waters to the Immense Water.

Conclusion

Passioning River

The journey on the River of Discovery to the Father of Waters was great, but it wasn't complete. That awareness intensified throughout the fall and winter, refusing to be dissolved. The four-legged canoe trip down the Wisconsin River with my sons was finished, but the voyage hadn't come to the fullness of its end.

Deep down, I sensed the solution. The circle had not been wholly drawn around the experience. The journey needed to return to its origins, to its beginning, to its source.

So finally around Easter, I asked my wife, Stephanie, if she wanted to join me the next summer on one more leg of the Russell River Rendezvous. You might remember that I started the journey with my son David at Prairie du Sac, just south of the last dam on the river. However, that meant that the first section of Marquette's journey, which started twenty-five miles north of this point, at the city of Portage, had not been reduplicated. Steph agreed to complete the circle with me.

Before Steph and I begin this final segment of the canoe voyage, we drive to the mile-and-a-quarter portage trail that the Marquette-Jolliet band, led by their two Miami guides, hiked with their canoes and supplies from the Fox River to the River of Discovery. In the 1850s a canal was built to join these two rivers, commingling their waters, but the canal is no longer used and its large iron gates have been permanently shut. So now the original order has been restored. The waters that run into the Fox flow into the Great Lakes and to the Atlantic Ocean by way of the St. Lawrence Seaway, while those flowing into the Wisconsin journey to the Mississippi and join the sea through the Gulf of Mexico. So this is liminal land, the threshold between two ways to the Immense Water.

Like many couples, Steph and I also walk on in-between space. Our first son is now firmly established in his adult life. Our youngest son is a freshman at the high school that bears Marquette's name. It will not be long before all of them are launched on their own careers and families to start the circle all over again. Our sons' ways into life's ocean may flow by paths much different than our own, but we hope they are people infused with a powerful passion for life, a passion that imbues their lives with purpose and meaning.

When I say *passion,* I am referring neither to simply sexual energy nor specifically excessive emotion. Rather, I mean the kind of passion that is an intense, driving, overmastering *affection for life.* It is an animated wisdom. "Passion people" are those whose spirits are tapped into a certain stillness, a peacefulness. These people are not pious types walking around with their heads in the clouds. Rather, they usually are pretty earthy; they sometimes tell off-color jokes and always seem to laugh from their guts. They are the type of person you want at your party because you know you will have a good time with them...and you also want them around when you are in pain, because they know the sacredness of our wounds and so provide fitting words of comfort. These people *choose* life. They embody the essence of Ephesians 2:4–5: "God...made us alive!"

I have concluded that passion people have a "seventh sense" that is undeveloped in the rest of us. What do I mean by a seventh sense? We all know about our five senses (sight, touch, smell, taste, and hearing), and we also talk about some people having a sixth sense, which is the ability to predict or have a premonition about the future. It seems to me that some people have another sense, a seventh sense, that gives them a capacity to see God's glorious presence and active love being outpoured in the every-dayness of life.

Passion people know they are living in a universe of love. They gratefully see that they are made and placed by our Triune God, who fashions us in the divine image, to seek, through our human desires, God's will for us...which is simply to live in love. They understand that they are called to be most fully what they are intended to be when they actualize their capacity to love through their life vocation. They have been pierced with the wounds of the world, but they feel and extend the wombful compassion of our mothering God. They know that they are not just made but embraced, and they love God by caring for God's creation and by loving others with a self-giving love. Oh, how they love! It is a wholehearted, fully embodied love.

I like to think of this passion as a *seventh* sense because in the Bible the number seven is always a symbol of completeness and perfection, like when God made the world in seven days. Seventh-sense people seem more "complete" and whole than the average. You could say this seventh sense is the ability to see God in all things, and this seems to stem from the fact that they live life at the *core* of the human imagination, which is the heart of integrity and the soul of love.

Passion people are people of gratitude who laugh from their guts, have an overmastering affection for life, know about the sacredness of wounds, see the glory of God emanating through all things, love ardently, live in the heart of the human imagination. In short, they follow Saint Paul's injunction to "put on Christ."

Ever-Changing River

After seeing this land bridge between the waters that Marquette traveled all those centuries ago, Steph and I drive back to the

Wisconsin River. We unload the canoe and place it in the river. As we stand knee-deep in the moving waters, the wise words of the Greek philosopher, Heraclitus (540–480 BCE), are most appropriate: "You do not step twice into the same river; for other waters are ever-flowing on to you." Through this metaphor, Heraclitus strove to teach that all things are in flux, that the one constant in life is change. Superficially, a river may appear stable and permanent, but an attentive observer sees that it is continually moving. It is not the same river from one moment to the next. The waters that pass by you one moment are not the same waters that flow by during the next; the shoreline and riverbed are also in a continual dance of dissolving, shifting, and moving. So too, then, is everything else in the world constantly becoming something else. If nothing else, every created thing is going from existence to out-of-existence.

Saint Francis de Sales also knew this underlying lesson. He goes beyond the truth that Heraclitus grasped, for he sees God's very tracings within the world's ever-moving changes. For Francis, change is the medium through which God interacts with the world and with us:

> God maintains the world in existence in a state of continual change: day passes into night, spring into summer, summer into autumn, autumn into winter, and winter into spring, and no two days are ever exactly alike, some being cloudy, some rainy, some dry, some windy, a variety which makes the world all the more beautiful. The same law of change applies to the human being, who has been called "an epitome of the world," for his state is ever changing, constantly in movement; his life on earth like waters which ebb and flow, sometimes lifted up by hope, sometimes depressed by fear, swept one way by consolation, another by affliction; no day, no hour, exactly the same. (Saint Francis de Sales, *Introduction to the Devout Life*, 223)

Some hear this assessment about the human condition and panic, buck, and reject this understanding of life. If all is in flux, what is dependable? If life is change, what is permanent? If existence is fading, what is eternal? If order is shifting, what is right?

Here is the good news: ours is a God of movement. God conforms God's very self to fill in our gaps. God infuses creation with an effusive grace that spills over, runs out, and soaks through all of life. Grace walks in the driest of lands to accompany us back through the water; it refreshes our souls with living waters that draw us to eternal life. Yes, ours is a Triune God whose divine essence, the irreducible core, is dynamically relational: Father, Son, and Holy Spirit. Our God exists as a dance among three persons who are eternally dancing—swirling, dipping, swaying, twirling. Ah, there is the heart of it: God as dance and dancing.

This is why the God Questions are so important. Every time we immerse ourselves in the current of the God Questions, we become aware of the subtle movements and surprising variations in God's response to our awkward missteps, stumbling efforts, exhausted energy, and hopeful actions. Engaging the God Questions refreshes, renews, and reintegrates us in the really real. Their contractions birth us into new life on the River of Discovery. So we must continually ask:

What is our place in the world?
Who is God calling us to be?
How is God caring for us?
Where is God's love?

Living within the God Questions bears us to the Father of Waters so that someday we might fully enter into the Immense Water of eternal life. They bear us to this Ultimate End because it is through the asking of questions that we most profoundly initiate and sustain conversations, and communication dissolves us into communion.

In the end, the story of our relationship with God is one of the oldest types of stories: it's a love story. Love is not a static object, but a dynamic energy. This means love is an ever-moving, ever-flowing, ever-infusing force. In fact, love can only exist as a convergence, an interaction, an inner penetration, a communion. This is why Pope Benedict XVI says:

> Acknowledgment of the living God is one path towards love, and the "yes" of our will to his will unites our intellect, will and sentiments in the all-embracing act of love. But this process is always open-ended; love is never "finished" and complete; throughout life, it changes and matures, and thus remains faithful to itself....The love-story between God and man consists in the very fact that this communion of will increases in a communion of thought and sentiment, and thus our will and God's will increasingly coincide: God's will is no longer for me an alien will, something imposed on me from without by the commandments, but it is now my own will, based on the realization that God is in fact more deeply present to me than I am to myself. Then self-abandonment to God increases and God becomes our joy (cf. *Ps* 73 [72]:23–28). (*DCE* 17)

God's loving presence moves in our lives and shapes who we are in very different ways at various points in our lives. Thus, God's love might very well mold us into new forms every time we seriously ask and engage the God Questions.

Questions are always agents of movement because their very nature requires, beckons, elicits, draws forth a response. And faith is a *response*. Not an answer. Not certitude. Not self-assurance. Not self-righteousness. Just a response. A response of gratitude. A response of desire. A response of compassion. A response of self-giving. In short, love.

The life of faith is a life lived on the river of questions. But we go forward with great confidence into the unknown because we have an innate God-wardness, and this God-wardness is drawing us toward love. Since God is love and we were made by God—in love—then our internal compass always points toward and is attracted toward love...that is, God. Thus we need not fear the questions for God is always with us. We just follow Jesus Christ, the Morning Star.

As Steph and I leap into the canoe and push off from shore, the summer-south sunlight plays on the water's ripples, glimmering and sparkling. With exchanged smiles, we turn the prow downriver, reach our paddles deeply into the dancing waters, and join our efforts with the river's generous current. Borne forth in love, we move forward in utter happiness, being dissolved into something complete and great.

Permissions and Bibliography

Permissions

Pope Benedict XVI: Excerpts from God Is Love *(Deus Caritas Est),* ©
2006, used with permission of Libreria Editrace Vaticana.

David L. Fleming, S. J.: Excerpts from *Draw Me Into Your Friendship:
A Literal Translation and a Contemporary Reading,* © 1996, copy-
righted and published by the Institute of Jesuit Sources, St. Louis, MO.
All rights reserved. Used with permission.

David L. Fleming, S. J.: Excerpts from *Like the Lightning: The Dynamics
of the Ignatian Exercises,* © 2004, copyrighted and published by the
Institute of Jesuit Sources, St. Louis, MO. All rights reserved. Used with
permission.

Michael Harter, S. J., editor: Excerpts from *Hearts on Fire: Praying With
Jesuits,* © 1993, copyrighted and published by the Institute of Jesuit
Sources, St. Louis, MO. All rights reserved. Used with permission.

Gerard Manley Hopkins: "God's Grandeur," from *Poems of Gerard
Manley Hopkins,* edited by W. H. Gardner and N. H. MacKenzie.
Oxford: Oxford University Press, 1970. Used by permission of Oxford
University Press, on behalf of the English Province of the Society of
Jesus.

International Committee on English in the Liturgy, Inc.: The English
translation of the Memorial Acclamation from *The Roman Missal,*
© 1974, International Committee on English in the Liturgy, Inc. All
rights reserved.

Denise Levertov: "The Avowal," from *Oblique Prayers,* © 1984 by Denise
Levertov. Reprinted by permission of New Directions Publishing Corp.

Henry Nouwen: Excerpt from *the Inner Voice of Love,* © 1996, used with
permission of Random House, Inc.

Ronald Rolheiser: Excerpts from *The Holy Longing: The Search for a Christian Spirituality,* © 1999, used with permission of Random House, Inc.

Tom and Dick Smothers: Excerpts from "Cabbage" skit adapted by Tom
and Dick Smothers, copyright Rave Music Inc. Used by permission.

Brian Swimme: Excerpt from *The Universe Is a Green Dragon: A Cosmic
Creation Story,* used by permission of Inner Traditions, Rochester, VT.
Copyright © 1984 by Brian Swimme. www.innertraditions.com.

Elisabeth Meier Tetlow, translator: Excerpt from "Principle and
Foundation" in *The Spiritual Exercises of St. Ignatius Loyola,* ©
1987 by University Press of America, Landham, Maryland. Used by
permission.

Bibliography

The sources listed below have been used in the writing of this book. The bibliography does not list all the consulted works and sources.

Adam, August. *The Primacy of Love.* Translated by E. C. Noonan. Westminster, MD: Newman Press, 1958.

Akerlund, Nels, and Joe Glickman. *Our Wisconsin River: Border to Border.* Rockford, IL: Pamacheyon Publishing, 1997.

Benedict XVI. *God Is Love/Deus Caritas Est.* December 25, 2005. Vatican City: Libreria Editrice Vaticana, 2006.

Birmingham, Robert A., and Leslie E. Esenberg. *Indian Mounds of Wisconsin.* Madison, WI: University of Wisconsin Press, 2000.

Borg, Marcus J. *Meeting Jesus Again for the First Time: The Historical Jesus and the Heart of Contemporary Faith.* San Francisco, CA: HarperSanFrancisco, 1994.

Bradley, H. Cornell, S. J. *The 19th Annotation in 24 Weeks, for the 21st Century.* Philadelphia, PA: St. Joseph's University Press, 2002.

Beuchner, Fredrick. *Wishful Thinking: A Theological ABC.* New York: Harper & Row, 1973.

Cather, Willa. *My Antonia.* Lincoln, NE: University of Nebraska Press, 1994.

Derleth, August. *The Wisconsin: River of a Thousand Isles.* New York: Farrar & Rinehart, 1942.

De Sales, Francis. *Introduction to the Devout Life.* Translated by M. Day. London: Burns & Oates, 1956.

Donnelly, Joseph P., S. J. *Jacques Marquette, S. J., 1637–1675.* Chicago, IL: Loyola University Press, 1968.

Dulles, Avery. "John Paul II and the Truth about Freedom." *First Things* 55 (1995): 3641.

Durbin, Richard D. *The Wisconsin River: An Odyssey through Time and Space.* Cross Plains, WI: Spring Freshet Press, 1997.

English, John J., S. J. *Spiritual Freedom,* 2nd ed., rev. and updated. Chicago, IL: Loyola University Press, 1995.

Fleming, David L., S. J. *Draw Me Into Your Friendship: The Spiritual Exercises—A Literal Translation and a Contemporary Reading.* St. Louis, MO: Institute of Jesuit Sources, 1996.

———. *Like the Lightning: The Dynamics of the Ignatian Exercises.* St. Louis, MO: Institute of Jesuit Sources, 2004.

———. *The Spiritual Exercises of Saint Ignatius: A Literal Translation and a Contemporary Reading.* St. Louis, MO: Institute of Jesuit Sources, 1978.

Fromm, Erich. *Man for Himself: An Inquiry Into the Psychology of Ethics.* Greenwich, CT: Fawcett Publications, 1947.

Hamilton, Raphael. N., S. J. *Father Marquette.* Grand Rapids, MI: Eerdmans, 1970.

———. *Marquette's Explorations: The Narratives Reexamined.* Madison, WI: University of Wisconsin Press, 1970.

Harter, Michael, S. J., ed. *Hearts on Fire: Praying With Jesuits.* St. Louis, MO: Institute of Jesuit Sources, 1993.

Hopkins, Gerard Manley, S. J. "God's Grandeur." In *The Poems of Gerard Manley Hopkins,* 4th ed., rev. and enl., edited by W. H. Gardner and N. H. MacKenzie. Oxford: Oxford University Press, 1970.

Kenton, Edna, ed. *The Jesuit Relations and Allied Documents: Travels and Explorations of the Jesuit Missionaries in North America (1610–1791).* New York: Vanguard Press, 1954.

Lehner, Ulrich. "Improper Wisdom: What a Pope Learned from August Adam." *Commonweal* 134, no. 2 (January 26, 2007): 15–18.

Leopold, Aldo. *A Sand County Almanac, and Sketches Here and There.* New York: Oxford University Press, 1989.

Levertov, Denise. "The Avowal." In *Selected Poems,* edited by P. A. Lacey. New York: New Directions Books, 2002.

Mann, Charles C. *1491: New Revelations of the Americas Before Columbus.* New York: Alfred A. Knopf, 2005.

Mark Link, S. J. *Challenge: A Meditation Program Based on the Spiritual Exercises of Saint Ignatius.* Valencia, CA/Allen, TX: Tabor Publishing, 1988.

———. *Challenge: A Daily Meditation Program Based on the Spiritual Exercises of Saint Ignatius.* Allen, TX: Thomas More, 1993.

Marquette, Jacques, S. J. "Journal." In *The Jesuit Relations: Natives and Missionaries in Seventeenth-Century North America,* edited by A. Greer. Boston/New York: Bedford/St. Martin's, 2000.

Metcoff, Jill. *Along the Wisconsin Riverway.* Madison, WI: University of Wisconsin Press, 1997.

Miller, Robert J., ed. *The Complete Gospels: Annotated Scholars Version.* San Francisco: HarperSanFrancisco, 1994.

Miller, William D. *A Harsh and Dreadful Love: Dorothy Day and the Catholic Worker Movement.* 2nd edition. Milwaukee, WI: Marquette University Press, 2005.

Moore, James T. *Indian and Jesuit: A Seventeenth-Century Encounter.* Chicago, IL: Loyola University Press, 1982.

Nouwen, Henri. *The Inner Voice of Love.* New York: Doubleday Publishers, 1996.

O'Leary, J. J., S.J., "A Short Course on Prayer." In *Accompaniment: The Integration of Faith/Prayer/Daily Life,* edited by J. M. Ewens. Milwaukee, WI: Ignatian Task Force Press, 1991.

Rahner, Karl. *Foundations of Christian Faith: An Introduction to the Idea of Christianity.* Translated by William V. Dych. New York: Crossroads, 1987.

Repplier, Agnes. *Pere Marquette: Priest, Pioneer and Adventurer.* Garden City, NY: Doubleday, Doran & Company, 1929.

Rohr, Richard. *Everything Belongs: The Gift of Contemplative Prayer.* New York: Crossroads, 1999.

Rolheiser, Ronald. *The Holy Longing: The Search for a Christian Spirituality.* New York: Doubleday, 1999.

Russell, Edmund P., Jr. "My Sun." In *Hymns of the Omaha Yoga School,* edited by M. Hahn. Omaha, NE: Pony Creek Press, 1997.

Stark, William F. *Wisconsin, River of History.* Self-published, 1988.

Svob, Mike. *Paddling Southern Wisconsin: 82 Great Trips by Canoe and Kayak.* Black Earth, WI: Trails Books, 2001.

Swimme, Brian. *The Universe Is a Green Dragon: A Cosmic Creation Story.* Santa Fe, MN: Bear & Company, 1984.

Tekiela, Stan. *Birds of Wisconsin: Field Guide.* 2nd ed. Cambridge, MN: Adventure Publications, 2004.

Tetlow, Elisabeth Meier, trans. *The Spiritual Exercises of Saint Ignatius of Loyola.* Lanham, MD: University Press of America, 1987.

Tetlow, Joseph, S. J. *Choosing Christ in the World.* St. Louis, MO: Institute of Jesuit Sources, 1989.

Thwaites, Reuben G. *Father Marquette.* New York: D. Appleton & Company, 1902.

————, ed. *Voyages of Marquette.* In *The Jesuit Relations and Allied Documents.* Vol. 59 by Jacques Marquette with French and English Text. Ann Arbor, MI: University Microfilms, Inc., 1966.

Trible, Phyllis. *God and the Rhetoric of Sexuality.* Philadelphia: Fortress Press, 1978.

United Nations Intergovernmental Panel on Climate Change. "Climate Change 2007," (Fourth Assessment Report, April 6, 2007).

Young, William J., transl. *St. Ignatius' Own Story.* Chicago: Loyola University Press, 1998.